THE BRIDE OF QUIETNESS
AND OTHER PLAYS

LONDON: HUMPHREY MILFORD
OXFORD UNIVERSITY PRESS

THE BRIDE OF
QUIETNESS

AND OTHER PLAYS

OSCAR W. FIRKINS

THE UNIVERSITY OF MINNESOTA PRESS
MINNEAPOLIS

TED BY THE COPYRIGHT LAWS
RADIO BROADCASTING, PUBLIC
TATION OF ANY KIND MAY BE
ITTEN PERMISSION OF
MINNESOTA PRESS
POLIS

932 BY THE
UNIVERSITY OF MINNESOTA

MADE IN THE UNITED STATES OF AMERICA

EDITOR'S NOTE

The plays contained in this and the succeeding volume were among those left by Professor Firkins at the time of his death in March, 1932. He had prepared them for publication and they are now presented, with only very slight exceptions, exactly as he left them. The author would doubtless have made some changes in the process of revision, but the editors have thought it best to leave his posthumous work as it came from his hand.

The Bride of Quietness, the title play in this volume, is, as readers will immediately recognize, the dramatist's imaginary history of Keats's " Ode on a Grecian Urn." In constructing a fantasy of this kind the author has, admittedly, exercised the traditional poetic license with both facts and probabilities. Throughout the five scenes of the play, the Grecian Urn itself is the real central figure. Yet, as Sidney Colvin says, " It is no single or actually existing specimen of Attic handicraft that he [Keats] celebrates in this ode, but a composite conjured up instinctively in his mind out of several such known to him in reality or from engravings." Other Keats critics are agreed in this opinion.

CONTENTS

THE BRIDE OF QUIETNESS

ODE ON A GRECIAN URN

1

Thou still unravish'd bride of quietness,
  Thou foster-child of silence and slow time,
Sylvan historian, who canst thus express
  A flowery tale more sweetly than our rhyme:
What leaf-fring'd legend haunts about thy shape
    Of deities or mortals, or of both,
      In Tempe or the dales of Arcady?
    What men or gods are these? What maidens loth?
What mad pursuit? What struggle to escape?
    What pipes and timbrels? What wild ecstasy?

2

Heard melodies are sweet, but those unheard
  Are sweeter; therefore, ye soft pipes, play on;
Not to the sensual ear, but, more endear'd,
  Pipe to the spirit ditties of no tone:
Fair youth, beneath the trees, thou canst not leave
    Thy song, nor ever can those trees be bare;
      Bold Lover, never, never canst thou kiss,
Though winning near the goal — yet, do not grieve;
    She cannot fade, though thou hast not thy bliss,
    For ever wilt thou love, and she be fair!

3

Ah, happy, happy boughs! that cannot shed
  Your leaves, nor ever bid the Spring adieu;
And, happy melodist, unwearied,
  For ever piping songs for ever new;

More happy love! more happy, happy love!
 For ever warm and still to be enjoy'd,
  For ever panting and for ever young;
All breathing human passion far above,
 That leaves a heart high-sorrowful and cloy'd,
  A burning forehead, and a parching tongue.

4

Who are these coming to the sacrifice?
 To what green altar, O mysterious priest,
Lead'st thou that heifer lowing at the skies,
 And all her silken flanks in garlands drest?
What little town by river or sea shore,
 Or mountain-built with peaceful citadel,
  Is emptied of this folk, this pious morn?
And, little town, thy streets for evermore
 Will silent be; and not a soul to tell
  Why thou are desolate, can e'er return.

5

O Attic shape! Fair attitude! with brede
 Of marble men and maidens overwrought,
With forest branches and the trodden weed;
 Thou, silent form, dost tease us out of thought
As doth eternity: Cold Pastoral!
 When old age shall this generation waste,
  Thou shalt remain, in midst of other woe
Than ours, a friend to man, to whom thou say'st,
 " Beauty is truth, truth beauty," — that is all
  Ye know on earth, and all ye need to know.

JOHN KEATS

THE BRIDE OF QUIETNESS

CHARACTERS IN SCENE I

PHILOTAS, *a Greek sculptor*   DIPHILUS, *a hunter*

CHARES, *a priest*   CHIONE, *a maiden*

EURYBATES, *a flute player*

OTHER GREEKS, MEN AND WOMEN

Place: a "little town" in the Vale of Tempe. Time: fourth century B.C.

Studio of Philotas. A wide opening at back reveals a small Greek village backed by steep and lofty hills.

A large urn, complete, but without decoration, in the foreground. Philotas with his chisel beside the urn; Chione posing to the left of the rear opening. It is early morning. Gay music from without.

CHIONE (*dropping her poised arms*).

The pipe! The timbrel!

PHILOTAS

Do not drop your arm.

CHIONE

The town goes fieldward. I must join the town.

⇢ 5 ⇠

PHILOTAS

Leave towns to — townsfolk. (*He comes to her, and rearranges her pose, not heeding her protests.*)

CHIONE (*stamping her little foot*).

You shall let me go.

PHILOTAS

What seeks the village in the fields today?

CHIONE

They sacrifice a heifer to the gods. (*Music again.*)
There will be dance and feasting. Let me go. (*She again tries to free herself, but Philotas, with a gentle obstinacy, persists in his rearrangements of her pose.*)
You are so rough, Philotas — care for naught
But what your hands can chisel, not for me.
If I were stone, you would be tenderer.

PHILOTAS

If you were stone, you would not run away.
Surely you love me.

CHIONE

If I did, what then?
Surely you would not have me lose the feast
Because I love you.

PHILOTAS

With the urn and you

I should not miss Olympus.

CHIONE

Diphilus

Had said "With me," not "With his bow and me,"
Fond though he be of hunting.

PHILOTAS

Has the chase

Taught gentler words than mine to Diphilus?
Has Eros twined his bowstring? Stay with me,
And I will carve a feast upon this stone
That shall outlast the sunset, face the dawn,
And with undulled, unweariable foot
Bind eves and morns together.

CHIONE (*shyly*).

If I stay,

Will *you* dance with me?

PHILOTAS

What! With work to do

Crave respite for these dedicated hands?
Let jealous urn and frowning chisel wait
Till I be sick of folly?

CHIONE

As you will.

Unchid by urn or chisel I shall go.
The whole town goes — even Lalage who sees

Dusk in mid-noon, and Laches, sunk in years,
Who shivers in the neighborhood of flame. (*Music
again. Chione looks through the opening.*)

PHILOTAS

The whole town will be still; I shall be still;
The chisel only, as it moves, will speak;
And from its edge will joyous silences
Take shape upon the rondure of the urn.

CHIONE

What do you mean by joyous silences?

PHILOTAS

Dumb lovers, players on the soundless flute,
And pausers in the dance whose lifted heel
Yearns for the irrecoverable ground.

CHIONE

And, having these, Philotas, why want me,
Whose joy is never tongueless?

PHILOTAS

                    I am young,
And sometimes think of other things than art.
At twenty, in the springtime, one is man.

CHIONE (*archly*).

But twenty?

PHILOTAS (*smiling*).
             Do I seem so old to you?

Twenty fleets fast — with oh, such crowding years
Wherein *not* to be twenty, nor be loved!

CHIONE

Come, then.

PHILOTAS

You, stay.

CHIONE

Come! (*Philotas shakes his
head.*) Come unto the feast.
I am not very fond of Diphilus.

PHILOTAS

Nay, nay, we shall be happier apart.
Had I been dearer to you than the feast,
Had you been dearer to me than the urn,
All had been well — nay, all *is* well. — Goodbye.
At eve come back — *come back with Diphilus,*
And you shall see your figure on the urn.

CHIONE (*interested*).

What shall I be?

PHILOTAS

What should you be? A girl —
A girl in love — lips rounded to a kiss.

CHIONE (*dropping her eyes*).

Whose kiss?

PHILOTAS (*looking at her*).

    Mine — had you questioned me at dawn:
But now — the lover shall be Diphilus.

CHIONE (*low-voiced*).

Their lips shall meet?

PHILOTAS (*suddenly*).

          By Zeus, they shall not meet!
The living lips I may not, would not part,
But these in stone whereof I am arbiter
They shall approach forever, never meet.
So far — not further than a cirque of stone
I push my rancor against Diphilus.

CHIONE

Philotas, look! They come! (*Philotas follows her to
the rear opening, whence, to the quickening pace
of the music, moving figures in holiday attire become imperfectly, but brightly, visible.*) Chares
is there.

PHILOTAS

He leads the heifer.

CHIONE

        White as his own beard.

PHILOTAS

Half Parian already. Round her horns
And thighs are garlands. Booty for my urn.

CHIONE

There is Eurybates, the flute player.

PHILOTAS

He shall to the urn. The flute shall make no sound,
But yet the air shall vibrate.

CHIONE

Brasidas —

The timbrel in his fingers.

PHILOTAS

More and more —

Vintagers, woodsmen — maidens in that flight
Which chases the pursuer. There he comes.

CHIONE

He?

PHILOTAS

Diphilus.

CHIONE

I saw him not.

PHILOTAS

He comes.

(*Enter Diphilus, followed by Eurybates and
Chares, who stop in the doorway. Chares has a
wreath in his hands.*)

DIPHILUS

Stay you, Chione? All the town's afoot.

The morn is like a trumpet. Forth, it cries.

CHIONE (*very briefly*).

I come. (*She moves toward the door.*)

EURYBATES

Be quick, Philotas.

PHILOTAS

I shall stay.

CHARES

Son, come with us.

CHIONE

He does not love our feasts.
Feasts ripen on his chisel.

CHARES

But the gods—
They go with us.

PHILOTAS

Apollo stays with me.

DIPHILUS

We stay, we stay. Shall all the world be sad,
Because one peevish fellow hugs his pain?

PHILOTAS

Peevish! We shall be happy both of us;
Each as he fancies—you in the peopled wild,
I in the speechless and dispeopled town.

THE BRIDE OF QUIETNESS

DIPHILUS

Come—to the feast! (*All but Philotas go out. Chione does not turn to look at Philotas, but, in a woman's by-play, takes the wreath from Chares as she passes out. Philotas looks after them for a pensive instant, then takes up his chisel and begins to work upon the urn. Chione, reappearing in the doorway, suddenly flings the wreath across his shoulders. He turns, sees her, and, moving suddenly toward her, is about to press his lips to hers, when, with a quick, vivacious gesture, she evades him. In the doorway she turns again.*)

CHIONE

The wreath for you, the kiss for Diphilus!

CURTAIN

CHARACTERS IN SCENE II

PHILOTAS   DIOCLES, *his servant*

URN FIGURES

SHAPE OF DIPHILUS   SHAPE OF CHARES
SHAPE OF CHIONE   SHAPE OF EURYBATES

OTHER SHAPES

The scene is forty years later, in a house in the Piraeus.
Philotas, an old man, is dying in his moonlit chamber.
The urn is in the room. Diocles enters.

PHILOTAS (*raising his head*).

What say they, Diocles?

DIOCLES

They are content.
The urn shall pass into the vault with you.

PHILOTAS

I take a little of this scant last breath
To thank them; I shall thank them in the grave,
If thankfulness outlive the heart and tongue.

DIOCLES (*looking at the urn figures*).

The world will miss them.

PHILOTAS

I should miss them more.

DIOCLES (*hesitatingly*).

The moon is bright, and yet the shapes are dim.
There is not even moonlight in the grave.
How will you see them?

PHILOTAS

                 Not with eyes or lamps.

Eyeless and torchless, still the artist sees
His own creations. Verily, if I wake,
They will be there. Who knows? — the *being there*
May wake me. When I am cold and still like them,
Will they not feel that they are kin to me?
Will they not leave their eminence, descend
From their high peace and wave their arms and
    dance,
If but to mock me with their nimbleness?
Would they blow jeering trumpets in my ear?
And would the girl there lift her daffodil,
And hold it to my nostril as she smiled,
Scarce knowing if she smiled in scorn of me
Or welcome to her lover?

DIOCLES

               I scarce think

That she would smile to ridicule the dead.
She has a kind face.

PHILOTAS

She is young, she loves,

And she is loved. Why should she not be kind?
Go to the urn — a mist obscures my sight —
And tell me if her lover's lips touch hers.

DIOCLES (going to the urn).

Not quite.

PHILOTAS (smiling).

Not quite? Not yet? He is the patientest

Of lovers. Unrequited! Forty years!
Diocles, should you one day pass my grave,
And hear a laughter seeping through the stones,
Be certain that I think of Diphilus.

DIOCLES

I should not laugh in passing by your grave,
Not though the grave were merry.

PHILOTAS

You would grieve?

I thank you. Grief is fugitive — and rare.
How long would blow the windflower on a grave,
If all its water fell from dropping eyes?
Few were the smiles in Hades — very few,
If the ghost smiled but when a tear were shed
To mark its passing. But I talk too much.
Go to your rest — as I shall go to mine.

DIOCLES

I would not leave you lonely.

PHILOTAS (*pointing to the figures on the urn*).

They are here. (*Diocles looks at him wistfully for a moment, then goes out. Philotas looks at the urn.*)

They stand aloft in their high, stoic calm;
Their immortality is motionless;
Eternity, like a circlet, round their necks
Is claspèd — prized as little and as much
As any other circlet. What is prayer
To them? They turn unseeing, heartless eyes
On me, who am their father. The quick brain,
The arm that wrought them, lifted, would not win
One tremor from their eyelids. I shall die.
From that tall casement has the last of dawns
Looked on me; and the last of moons now looks
Upon this forehead and these idle hands.
Aloof, in their inscrutable repose,
They care not if the sound that cleaves the dark
Means that a mouse has perished or a man. (*A long silence.*)
If they would come — come even after death,
Come in some trance that mingles death with life,
If my great love could draw them — (*He sinks into*

THE BRIDE OF QUIETNESS

*a trance. Silence. The shapes on the urn begin to
waver.*)

SHAPE OF CHARES

He calls us.

SHAPE OF EURYBATES

We are summoned.

SHAPE OF THE TIMBREL PLAYER

We descend.

SHAPE OF DIPHILUS

To move, Chione!

SHAPE OF CHIONE

Diphilus! To move!

SHAPE OF A DANCER

To lift the never lifted ankle, sink
The never falling heel!

SHAPE OF ANOTHER DANCER

To bend the knee!

SHAPE OF EURYBATES

To see the leaflet quiver, see it *fall!*

SHAPE OF CHARES

To feel the heifer straining on the leash!

SHAPE OF A DANCER

To lose the sandal!

SHAPE OF ANOTHER DANCER

Find it, *put it on!*

SHAPE OF DIPHILUS

To touch one's forehead!

SHAPE OF CHIONE

To let loose one's hair!

SHAPE OF EURYBATES (*approaching Philotas*).

He sleeps.

SHAPE OF CHARES (*also approaching*).

He is our maker. (*All turn, but some less markedly than others, toward Philotas.*)

SHAPE OF A DANCER

He is old.

SHAPE OF CHARES

What skills it? When he made us, he was young.

SHAPE OF A DANCER (*surveying herself*).

Ah, well, I thank him for a comely wrist.

SHAPE OF ANOTHER DANCER (*also surveying herself*).

I for a dainty instep.

SHAPE OF CHARES

He was good

To bless me with a venerable beard.

SHAPE OF CHIONE (*to Shape of Diphilus*).

What do you thank him for?

SHAPE OF DIPHILUS

For you — for you;

For nearness — nearness in beloved lips —

I thank him. But for that stern interval,
The little cleft that a fly's wing could span,
The great cleft that the cycles could not bridge,
I chide the niggard.

SHAPE OF CHIONE (*in a low voice*).

Do you chide him *now?*

SHAPE OF DIPHILUS

Not now. The lips he set apart shall meet,
Meet in his presence. One long look and then —

SHAPE OF CHIONE

Haste lest he waken — lest he loose the spell.

SHAPE OF DIPHILUS

His sleep is peaceful. Dear, our moment comes,
Wrenched from the grasping ages. (*The two shapes,
having withdrawn from each other far enough
and long enough to exchange a look of mutual
anticipation, suddenly draw near.*)

PHILOTAS (*from the couch*).

No, not that.

Not that. Back to your couches in the stone! (*The
shapes of Chione and Diphilus sway toward each
other for an instant before they are caught in the
swift, recessive movement which sweeps the whole
group backward to their places on the urn. The
trance of Philotas has dissolved.*)

THE BRIDE OF QUIETNESS

The trance disperses. They are stone again.
They flee, each to his station; Diphilus,
Chione. And between their mutual thirst
The space, the small, inexorable space,
That flings its gauntlet to the centuries keeps
The warning of its presence. Never again
Shall they forsake their cold tranquillity,
Unless indeed some spirit, loving them
After my fashion, praying as I prayed,
Tempted them from their station. Futile dream!
Who loves them with *my* love? They shall go down
Into the shadow and the hush with me.
We shall embrace the stillness, they and I.
What should they be but stone when I am clay?
  (*He dies.*)

CURTAIN

CHARACTERS IN SCENE III

PERDIX, *a Greek water carrier* ENGLISH OVERSEER
MYRTO, *a fruit seller*   ENGLISH WORKERS, *not*
             speaking

More than two thousand years have passed. The scene is the harbor of Piraeus in 1812; the hour is noon. In the clear, wide bay that forms the background, an English ship, with bright white sail, is anchored. On the beach a small skiff. In the foreground at the left a wide excavation reaching far into the hillside; at the right, an enormous plane tree, offering a refuge from the heat in its broad shadow. Shrubbery — cornel, hazel, and acanthus — farther forward on the left. Front stage bare except for fragments of statues and the bases and tops of columns strewn about. On one of these bases sits Myrto, the fruit seller, her basket at her feet, her eyes gazing seaward. Perdix, standing above her on the slope, looks down discontentedly at her deep and still preoccupation. His water jar, full to the brim, is at his feet.

In the mouth of the excavation appear the English overseer and one workman. They carry carefully between their arms a nondescript object the shape of which is lost in grimy incrustations. Perdix and Myrto watch intently the placing of this object on the ground to left of center. At the sound of a horn, workmen pour forth from the excavation, and disperse themselves on the ground beneath the plane tree to eat their midday meal. Perdix offers water; they drink eagerly. Myrto offers figs, dates, and oranges; several buy. Having drunk and eaten, they fall asleep in picturesquely varied postures. The overseer, at left, propping his back against a broken statue, is the last to close his eyes. Myrto returns to her seat. Perdix lies on the ground before her feet. All is still.

PERDIX

Did they buy much? (*Myrto, without a word, opens her palm, and discloses a small heap of Greek and English coins.*) They give you English coins?

MYRTO (*indifferently, closing her palm*).

What matter? Greeks will take them.

PERDIX

All the Greeks?

MYRTO

To the last man. Though Britain has her foes,
The English sixpence and the English pound
Have not an enemy in all the world. (*She falls into new revery. Pause.*)

PERDIX (*edging nearer*).

Myrto, a kiss.

MYRTO (*with the half indulgent, half contemptuous tranquillity which marks all her ways with Perdix*).

I told you "No" last night.

PERDIX (*coaxingly*).

Noon is so far from night.

MYRTO

Not half so far

As "No" from "Yes."

PERDIX

Is "Yes" so very far?

Shall it be "Yes" tonight? (*Myrto shakes her head.*)
  Tomorrow, then?

What shall I do to earn a "Yes" from you?

MYRTO

Nothing. I do not love the mouths of Greeks.

PERDIX

Not when they sue to you?

MYRTO

I love their prayers

As little as their kisses.

PERDIX

Use a kiss

To end the prayers.

MYRTO

I end them with a date.

Content you. (*Puts a date into his mouth.*)

PERDIX (*eating*).

It is honey to the lips.

MYRTO

A Greek's heart is no larger than his mouth.

A date fills both. (*This with her unvaryingly good-natured slight.*)

PERDIX (*confused*).

If you had given the kiss—

MYRTO

The old vain prayer! Look, Perdix, at that sail.

While yonder ship is anchored in our bay,

I will not kiss a Greek.

PERDIX (*alarmed*).

Not kiss a Greek?

You love an English seaman?

MYRTO (*smiling*).

No, not I.

I do not love the spoilers—nor the spoiled.

PERDIX

They take our marble, but they give us gold.

MYRTO

They take the effigies of Zeus away,

And leave—a Briton's image on a coin.

PERDIX

We could not fight the English.

MYRTO

> Nor the Turks.

Greeks can but beg for kisses. There's a task
Matching their valor.

PERDIX

> Who can fight in chains?

MYRTO

Greeks cannot fight nor carve. The edgeless sword
Sleeps by the blunted chisel. Have you a knife?

PERDIX

I have. (*Shows knife.*)

MYRTO

> Good! It will serve.

PERDIX (*uneasily*).

> > Will serve for what?

MYRTO

I ask for nothing manly. Do not blench.

PERDIX

What, then?

MYRTO (*pointing to the nondescript object*).

> Cut from that shapeless thing the dirt.

I have a whim to let its native sun,
The Greek sun, rediscover its lost grace
Before it sails for England.

PERDIX

        I will try. (*He scrapes off the incrustations. Myrto watches him intently.*)

MYRTO

It is an urn — with carvings.

PERDIX (*working*).

                There are leaves,
Boughs, tree boles.

MYRTO (*musingly*).

             Leaves that never danced in spring
Nor quaked in autumn.

PERDIX (*working*).

               Legs, a horn, a tail!

MYRTO

A heifer garlanded for sacrifice.

PERDIX

And here are women, men, a girl who flees,
A dancer — many dancers — Myrto, see —
A player on the timbrel.

MYRTO

            On the flute.

PERDIX

A rustic feast day. Was it long ago?

MYRTO

Two thousand years — what know I? — more or less.

PERDIX

'Tis odd to think two thousand years ago
Men went to pleasant places in the fields
And wanted to be happy.

MYRTO

Men were men,
And spring was spring, two thousand years ago.

PERDIX (*at work again*).

Here are two lovers. Their lips join, I think.

MYRTO

Are you so sure? Take off that bit of clay.

PERDIX (*obeying*).

The lips are parted — parted in approach.

MYRTO (*drawing near, and looking intently*).

Parted for always! There can be no change.
In marble the beginning is the end.

PERDIX

The sculptor was a surly man. He left
Hope unfulfilled.

MYRTO

But yet he saved the hope.
Perhaps he was too tender to be kind.

PERDIX (*ending his work*).

The urn is beautiful.

MYRTO

A Greek has eyes,
But has not hands to chisel — or to hold.

PERDIX (*indicating the urn figures*).
And will they go to England, do you think?

MYRTO

The ship waits. When does England wait in vain?

PERDIX

And will they dance there — dance with thoughtless
heel —
To unregretful pipings — lustily?
Will other skies than ours be skies for them?

MYRTO (*in her old seat*).
Who shall prevent their going?

PERDIX (*noting the overseer and workmen*).
They are lost
In stupor. I might hide the precious thing.
This way — the thicket — next the tunnel — last
The cabin in the beech wood known to few.
Advise me, Myrto.

MYRTO (*looking strangely at him*).
If you take the urn,
The overseer will catch you.

PERDIX
But he sleeps.

MYRTO

I trust the sleep of overseers no more—(*here she
pauses, and looks at Perdix*)
Than a Greek's inclination to be brave.

PERDIX

Well, since you bid me stay—

MYRTO

                        I did not say
You should not go. I said that, if you went,
The overseer would catch you. (*Perdix looks at her
in amaze, then takes a sudden resolve.*)

PERDIX

                          Be it so.
I take the hazard. England shall not grasp
The urn, if one bold leap, one breathless run,
May save it. (*He springs forward, and lifts the urn
in his arms. But the overseer, no less rapid than
he, is already upon him. The urn is wrenched
from his hold, he is dashed to the ground by a
stinging and resistless blow. Myrto rises, but takes
no step.*)

THE OVERSEER

Dog! Thief! Take measure of your parent earth!
Here, Roger, Duncan! Rouse ye! Take this urn

Instantly to the skiff, thence to the ship! (*Two workmen come forward, lift the urn between them, and carry it to the boat. The others, roused by the call, sit up, and prepare to rise and redescend into the excavation. Meanwhile, Myrto, advancing, reaches a hand to Perdix. He struggles to his feet, his face battered and bleeding. Standing side by side, they watch the slow progress of the bearers of the urn. The skiff, having received the urn, is rowed slowly toward the ship. The hands of Perdix and Myrto seek each other.*)

MYRTO (*in a dry voice, turning her eyes away*).
I will kiss you if you like.

PERDIX

> Not now. Not now.

I am all one bruise. A dog would turn from me, Myrto.

MYRTO (*with passionate tenderness*).

It is the bruises that I kiss. (*Their lips meet. When they slowly draw apart, the skiff has reached the side of the English man of war, and the two oarsmen lift the urn across the side of the skiff into the larger vessel.*)

CURTAIN

CHARACTERS IN SCENE IV

JOHN KEATS   FANNY BRAWNE

URN FIGURES

SHAPE OF DIPHILUS   SHAPE OF EURYBATES
SHAPE OF CHIONE   OTHER SHAPES

Time: May, 1819. Scene: a corner of the British Museum toward nightfall. Amid other shapes and parts of shapes, the urn alone is distinctly visible toward right center. Window at left, looking out upon a busy London street; the lights and sounds from this street become more noticeable, as the museum itself grows dim and quiet with the falling day. Fanny Brawne is looking down into the street from the window. John Keats is on a settee at left front.

FANNY BRAWNE

It is too dim — I cannot see the clock —
Not clearly — it is half past five, I think.

JOHN KEATS

Who minds the clock? I love you.

FANNY BRAWNE

But I mind.

JOHN KEATS

When you are with me, Sweet, I jest at time,

And when you are not—

FANNY BRAWNE

Well?

JOHN KEATS

Time scoffs at me.

FANNY BRAWNE (*looking into the street*).

I am almost certain it is half past five.
The street is full of noises and of lamps.

JOHN KEATS

Who minds the street? I love you.

FANNY BRAWNE

And I you;

But when the dusk falls, one must know the hour.

JOHN KEATS

I know your lashes have a purple fringe,
And that is hour and day and month and year
And time and half eternity for me.

FANNY BRAWNE (*curiously*).

Sometimes I think you love me very much.

JOHN KEATS

And when you think I do not?

FANNY BRAWNE

Then I think

That one of those cold figures on the urn
Is quite as much alive for you as I.

THE BRIDE OF QUIETNESS

JOHN KEATS

I lend to them the life I take from you,
And love you in their semblance. They have ways
Prettier than yours. They like my company,
And never pester me about the time.

FANNY BRAWNE (rationally).

They do not go to balls.

JOHN KEATS (dreamily).

                  And yet they dance,
Dance in this dim museum, lustily
As in Greek meads two thousand years ago,
Dance for all England, dance for me, John Keats,
Whom no one thought of when their dance began.

FANNY BRAWNE

John, you should write a play and buy a watch.
There is no money in these books of verse,
Much as I love them.

JOHN KEATS

          If I wrote a play,
It would not be to buy myself a watch.

FANNY BRAWNE (in a lowered voice).

Not one for me, dear heart?

JOHN KEATS

                That you might learn
The surelier and the sooner when to go?

THE BRIDE OF QUIETNESS

FANNY BRAWNE

John, you mistake. I do not wish to go.
But there's the ball, the dinner, and the dress.
Staying, I should be late.

JOHN KEATS

              And if you were — ?

FANNY BRAWNE

Foolish! You men have not the faintest guess
How unforgiving hostesses can be.

JOHN KEATS

Fanny, sit here with me. (*Fanny does not refuse, but
she sits on the bare edge of the settee, and gives
him the hand for which he reaches with an air
of despatching the preliminaries to departure.*)
              I wish to write
An ode — a lyric — for the Grecian urn.
They (*he points to the urn figures*) stay with me —
are faithful. Will you stay?

FANNY BRAWNE

How should I help you, staying?

JOHN KEATS

                      With your hand.
I fold my warmth within your hand and dream,
And Castaly sends bubbles through my veins,

And lyrics, tendril-like, as from a vine,
Break from my forehead.

FANNY BRAWNE

You shall have my hand
Tomorrow.

JOHN KEATS

When the violins begin,
Do the feet say "Tomorrow?" Do you care
So little for my verses?

FANNY BRAWNE

But, my love,
I think your verses charming.

JOHN KEATS

Stay with me.
That shall be proof.

FANNY BRAWNE

I'll give you better proofs.
I know them, I repeat them. Wednesday last —
Or was it Friday at Sir Richard Dilke's? —
'Twas Friday at Sir Richard's — some of them
I quoted to my partner in the waltz.
What a girl quotes in waltzes, be assured,
She values. I can give the very words.
"Charmed magic casements over — jeweled lawns."
You knit your brows — ungrateful! I am sure

'Twas "casements." If it was not "jeweled lawns,"
'Twas something quite as pretty.

JOHN KEATS

                              In the waltz
Tonight I shall be thought of?

FANNY BRAWNE

                         Do not fear.
Once I shall think of you in every waltz,
Twice, if my partner has a double chin,
And three times if he tramples on my toes.

JOHN KEATS

You are very gamesome. Fanny, when in thought
I see you, *feel* you, in another's arms —
Not these arms, but another's — all is dim.
The lights quake, the floor totters, and I fall.
Then buried couch I underneath a stone,
And on the stone a little dancing foot
Goes tapping — tapping — tapping till the dawn.

FANNY BRAWNE

You make me shiver. Shall you talk like that
When we are married?

JOHN KEATS

                 When we marry, dear,
I sometimes think I shall not talk at all.

THE BRIDE OF QUIETNESS

FANNY BRAWNE

Shall I do all the talking? You scarce heed
What I say now.

JOHN KEATS

            I listen to the voice,
I listen to the voice, and slight the words.
Who marks the letters on a golden coin?

FANNY BRAWNE

My words are naught to you? I stay no more,
Lest I should teach you if the voice you love
Be musical in chiding. (*She rises.*)

JOHN KEATS

           Will you go?

FANNY BRAWNE (*playfully reproving*).
Dearest! (*Changing her tone.*) Come *you!*

JOHN KEATS (*pointing to the urn figures*).
                They keep me — and the ode.

FANNY BRAWNE (*approaching the urn in her
    leisurely movement toward the door*).
They are but dreams and shadows.

JOHN KEATS

                 When you go,
I shall be dream and shadow. Half I fear,
You gone, they will assert their fellowship,
Come down, possess me, bid me dwell with them

In the high immobility of stone.

FANNY BRAWNE

Would you pipe there or dance — or woo perhaps?
Are these not lovers?

JOHN KEATS

Yes.

FANNY BRAWNE

With lips that meet. (*Looking more closely.*)
John, they do *not* meet!

JOHN KEATS

No.

FANNY BRAWNE

How long ago

Was this urn carved?

JOHN KEATS

Two thousand years — or more.

FANNY BRAWNE

Two thousand years, and nothing gained by it.
A woman should not bid a man make haste,
But these Greek girls were patient.

JOHN KEATS

Boy and girl

Equally patient. Fanny, I could dream
These passionate shapes might earn one breath of
    life,

One breath, and age-long fealty might win
Its fleeting, bright requital in a kiss.

FANNY BRAWNE

You shall stay here, and woo them to descend.
I go. What shall I fetch you from the ball?
A sweetmeat? — Not a sweetmeat? — Then a rose.
A rose shall intercede and make it plain
That Fanny, though she dearly loves a waltz,
Is not averse to poets, rather likes
One poet, though he grumbles overmuch,
And would not keep him waiting for a kiss
More than a century. Dearest heart! Goodbye! (*She
puts her hands upon his shoulders, and kisses him
briefly, gayly, and saucily; then trips out of the
door with a buoyant farewell gesture. Keats fol-
lows her to the door, and then follows her descend-
ing figure with eye and ear. When the last glimpse
and sound have vanished, he comes back into the
room.*)

JOHN KEATS

The last sound. The last step on the last stair,
And silence is a gloom within the gloom. (*He goes
to the window and looks out.*)
If I could see her red scarf. — Better not.

✵ 40 ✵

Its folds would twine about my neck all night,
And morning would be cheated of its ode. (*Pause.*)
How the street twinkles, crisps, bubbles, and foams!
The dusk that stills the meadow wakes the street,
Wakes it to cheer. Night is its second day. (*Pause.*)
I, born of that, (*he points downward*) was born *to*
    that, and this. (*Gesture toward urn.*)
To this? (*Comes back into the room.*) Are we not
    brethren, I and they? (*Gesture toward figures.*)
Blitheness and stir beneath us. We remain
Lost in the greying dimness, they and I. (*Pause.*)
Blitheness and stir? The *stone* is blithe and stirs.
Greek morn and English eve — pipe, dance, and kiss.
These drops upon my forehead — English mist,
Or dew that shook upon the myrtle leaf
In old, bright times when Greece was virginal?
    (*Pause.*)
Who was their graver? Was he young? And fond
Of some gay Greek who loved him rather more
Than almonds, rather less than festivals?
He loved them. Do I love them less? He gave
Duration, fixity. Could I give more? (*Pause. He
    meditates profoundly.*)
He gave confinement. Should I grant release?
Turn captive into gipsy? If, perchance,

The beauty which he, loving, bound in stone
I, loving, freed in music? If I turned
This stone — set winter into lyric spring,
If to these shapes I, giving breath, gave wings,
To speed their eager passage round the world?
　　(*Pause.*)
Would they be grateful? Would they stir no foot,
Shift not an eyelash? Would the instant's joy
Propitiate the cycles, bring to pass
The long expected, never granted kiss,
The undispelled, the unfulfilled desire,
The hope uncrowned, undaunted? But I dream.
　　(*Pause.*)
Changes crowd fast upon me, I grow old,
Primeval, in this dimness. If the past
Be dusk, then twilight is antiquity. (*He sits on the
　　settee.*)
I faint, I dwindle. (*Looking at the figures.*) They
　　are near and warm. (*Pause.*)
What if the spirit of fire that leaves these veins
Rekindled theirs, if they awoke to taste
A tingling, fleeing, palpitating joy!
What if they drew me with persuasive hand!
I might go back with them to perished Greece,
Or, hand in hand with them, remount the urn,

And share their timeless glory — but for Her! (*He
looks at the shapes of Diphilus and Chione.*)
I yearn for their high quiet. Do they yearn
For warmth and motion? If they came to life,
What would they think of first? The kiss? Or me?
(*He falls into a trance. Pause. The silence becomes gradually charged with expectation. The
street lamps lighten the gloom a very little.
A change is perceptible in the urn figures, a
change which, at the beginning, is less than a stir,
less than a whisper. But the outlines in the stone
begin to lose even the faint substance they have
kept in the dusk; and other outlines in their likeness — their counterfeits in mist, or, possibly, in
flesh and blood — assume shape and matter and
identity, upon the floor. The dancers, timbrel
players, and fleeing maidens are the first to dis-
involve themselves from the pervasive shadow.
The shape of Eurybates becomes clear; then that
of Chares, which remains near the urn, as if to
watch the heifer. The last shapes to descend or to
emerge are those of Diphilus and Chione. There
is eager, though noiseless, movement among the
figures, and their voices, though low, quiver with
the exultation of release.*)

THE BRIDE OF QUIETNESS

A SHAPE

I breathe!

ANOTHER SHAPE

Kind Zeus! The ecstasy of breath!

A THIRD SHAPE

The happy and dilating nostril feels
The goad, the importunity, of air.

A FOURTH SHAPE

Are men unhappy who can breathe?

A FIFTH SHAPE

What need
Of flagons when the simple draught of air
Is nectar?

THE FIRST SHAPE

The ice melts in the frozen wrist.

THE SECOND SHAPE

And the long patience of the foot is blessed
With motion.

THE THIRD SHAPE

And the wonder of the ground!

THE FOURTH SHAPE

Is this air Grecian?

THE FIFTH SHAPE

Chares, do we wake
In Tempe or Piraeus? Tell us where.

THE BRIDE OF QUIETNESS

SHAPE OF CHARES

I am bereft of answers. From the tomb,
Sea-borne, to this dim, unprefigured isle,
We sped. I do not even guess its name.

THE FIRST SHAPE

Is its tongue Greek?

SHAPE OF CHARES

I have not heard its tongue.

FIRST SHAPE

I wonder do they venerate our gods?
Do altars fume to Hera and to Zeus?

THE SECOND SHAPE

Does sage Demeter watch the sprouting seed,
Or Dionysus fecundate the vine?

SHAPE OF CHARES (*pointing to John Keats*).
Perhaps this youth can tell us.

THE THIRD SHAPE

Look! He sleeps.
When — ages since — we last forsook the urn,
Philotas slept.

THE FOURTH SHAPE

Our maker — he was old.

THE FIFTH SHAPE

This man might be our wooer — he is young.

SHAPE OF CHARES

Not Grecian. Hellas did not mold that chin,
Or curb that wayward profile. But his look
Might well have pleased Apollo.

SHAPE OF CHIONE

Or delayed

Artemis for a second on her way
To tryst on Latmos with Endymion.

SHAPE OF DIPHILUS

These foreign youths attract you?

SHAPE OF CHIONE

Hark! He speaks.

JOHN KEATS (*in sleep*).

"For ever wilt thou love, and she be fair!"

SHAPE OF CHARES

Not Greek.

SHAPE OF EURYBATES

Yet musical to Grecian ears.

SHAPE OF CHIONE

The thought of Greece, perhaps the thought of *us,*
May have inspired that music.

SHAPE OF EURYBATES

Hark, again!

JOHN KEATS (*in sleep*).

"For ever warm and still to be enjoyed."

THE BRIDE OF QUIETNESS

SHAPE OF CHIONE

A voice that chants. The chisel fashioned us.
What if the chisel flung us to the lyre?

SHAPE OF CHARES

Sound is but air, and air is volatile;
Snatched from our moorings, wafted by that breath,
We should be voyagers about the world.

SHAPE OF A DANCER

We have been speechless. Be speech now our life!

SHAPE OF DIPHILUS

Dream you of him, Chione?

SHAPE OF CHIONE

He has dreamt,
Dreamt long and lovingly, I think, of us.
Else why, young, with youth's joy in fellowship,
Companionless, here in the dark, is he?

SHAPE OF DIPHILUS

Hear me. I waited twenty hundred years.
Entreaty never held its watch so long.
Do I wait still, Chione?

SHAPE OF CHIONE

Have *my* lips
Fainted in constancy? I kiss him first,
Then you.

SHAPE OF DIPHILUS

Him first?

SHAPE OF CHIONE

You last and dearest.

SHAPE OF DIPHILUS

Why

Waste moments? Twenty centuries should be
Counselors to swiftness.

SHAPE OF CHIONE

Let them rather be
Tutors in patience. From his boyish lips
I gather balms for yours.

SHAPE OF DIPHILUS

The instants prick
More keenly than the terraced centuries
But now.

SHAPE OF CHIONE

I have been, and I shall be, yours.
Wait. (*She stoops toward John Keats.*) Will you
mount with us upon the urn,
When you have made your song, your roving song,
That carries you with us around the world? (*She
kisses his lips.*)

JOHN KEATS

Upon the urn? No. (*Like one clutching at a*

thought as at a rope.) Fanny — Fanny Brawne!
(*He wakes. Chione turns instinctively, passion-
ately, to Diphilus, but the dissolving spell divides
their lips in the very act of meeting. The whole
group of urn figures are again swept as by a wind,
backward and upward, to their ancient places on
the urn.*)

FIRST SHAPE

My hair is loosened.

THE SECOND SHAPE

Is my sandal gone? (*John
Keats sits up, stands, walks to the urn, and con-
templates the figures, motionless in the twilight.*)

JOHN KEATS

I will not mount with them. Yet but for Her — (*He
turns, draws a pencil and tablet from his pocket,
seats himself on the window ledge to profit by the
street lamps, and writes rapidly.*)
"For ever panting, and for ever young." (*He looks
up.*)
I wonder in whose arms she dances now. (*He writes
again.*)
And under what intolerable eyes
The little ruby circlet at her throat

Shimmers and gleams. They touch her palm, and
live!
But to the work. The lines run pleasantly. (*He
writes eagerly.*)
"Who are these coming to the sacrifice?" (*Writes.*)
"Or mountain-built, with peaceful citadel,
Is emptied of this folk." (*He stops writing.*) What
if a rose
Fell from her bosom in the hurrying dance?
She would dance on, would tread it under foot,
Heedless, not minding that it was *her* rose.
The rose — that is my heart. But to the ode. (*Writes
swiftly.*)
The lines run very pleasantly, I think.
Even in the dark the words gleam. In the street
The lamps and all their gleamlets sink at dawn.
Suppose *this* gleam were immortality?
Who can be certain? In a faithless world
Who can be sure of tablet, mound, or urn?
No matter. One is certain of a grave.

CURTAIN

CHARACTERS IN SCENE V

The Curator of the British Museum

Roger, *watchman*

Visitor

The place is that of Scene Four. The time is ten o'clock in the morning of February twenty-fourth, 1821. Roger enters; raises first the curtain, then the window, letting in sunshine and fresh air. Then he returns to the door.

ROGER

This way, sir. (*The Visitor enters, followed by the Curator. Both are dignified men in the late fifties. Cry of "*Times*" in the street outside.*)

CURATOR

Very good. (*To the Visitor.*) This is the urn You brought to England. Roger, you may go. (*Roger starts.*)
Stay, fetch me up a copy of the *Times.*

ROGER

Here, sir?

CURATOR

Yes, here. (*Roger bows and leaves the room.*)

VISITOR

I recognize the stone.

CURATOR

During the voyage to England, as I hear,
You made a careful study of the urn.

VISITOR

Yes, I could draw it now from memory.

CURATOR

That is the reason why we seek your aid.
For two years back, or less, a sharp dispute,
A wrangle almost, has gone briskly on
Between the janitors who share the charge
Of this part of the building and the urn.

VISITOR

Their quarrels must be loud indeed to reach
Your office.

CURATOR

       They dispute about the urn.
Each thinks the other mad. The rest of us
Incline to credit both with lunacy.

VISITOR

What is the ground of quarrel?

CURATOR

              You observe
This dancer's head? The hair is loose.

VISITOR (*after a long and strangely meditative
pause*).

I see.
The snood no longer holds it.

CURATOR

Dick avers —
You will laugh, but his oaths are forcible —
That, when he first came here to work, the hair
Was held up by the snood.

VISITOR

The other man
Denies the saying?

CURATOR

Roger says that Dick
Is moonstruck. But here comes the curious thing —
Roger, a sturdy, steady, truthful man,
Has his own madness.

VISITOR

What has changed for him?

CURATOR

Notice that sandal.

VISITOR

It is off the foot. (*His tone is grave.*)

CURATOR

Roger says, when he started work with us,
The sandal was half on.

VISITOR

A curious fact.

CURATOR

Why not a curious falsehood? Dick himself
Admits that Roger's fancy is perverse.
Dick jeers at Roger, Roger scoffs at Dick.
Oath jostles oath, yet both are honest men,
And friendly to each other.

VISITOR

You believe

That they err?

CURATOR

I believe in common sense.

VISITOR

If so, what need of me?

CURATOR

To end their doubts —
Not to confirm my certainties.

VISITOR

You assume

That what I say must contradict their words?

CURATOR (*a little stiffly*).

I assume nothing but your sanity.

VISITOR (*smiling*).

And that, too, possibly with some reserves.

THE BRIDE OF QUIETNESS

One question. Do you ask me what I think,
Or just — what I remember? Am I here
As judge or witness?

> CURATOR (*stiffly again*).

> Witness, if you please.

> VISITOR

One question more. Can you endure surprise?

> CURATOR (*relaxing a very little*).

I prove it at this moment.

> VISITOR

> Very well.

Both men are right — precisely, wholly right
In the two points in which you call them mad.

> CURATOR (*indignant*).

What?

> VISITOR

> I remember clearly both details.

The sandal was half on, the hair was tied.

> CURATOR (*pointing to the urn*).

But look.

> VISITOR (*calmly*).

> I look.

> CURATOR

> Well, then?

THE BRIDE OF QUIETNESS

VISITOR

Well?

CURATOR (*his arm on the Visitor's coat sleeve*).

Dear sir,
Think of the implications.

VISITOR

The facts first.
Afterwards, at our leisure, if we choose,
Testing of implications.

CURATOR

The facts first?
The facts must square with reason.

VISITOR

I admit
Reason's supremacy in reason's field.
In memory reason's nothing but a quack.

CURATOR (*half bursting*).

I think this urn has an uncanny power
To —

VISITOR (*amused*).

To unhinge the human intellect?
My dear Curator, we must go at once.
Mania is costly. Your capacities
Are valuable to England.

CURATOR (*sensibly ignoring this*).
                    Reinspect
The urn, the figures. Are there other things
That contradict remembrance? (*The Visitor care-
fully surveys the urn.*)

                    VISITOR
                                    I observe
A crack here.

                    CURATOR (*surprised*).
            What? A crack?

                    VISITOR
                                    Beyond a doubt.

                    CURATOR
But that is new.

                    VISITOR
                    You asked for novelties.
A crack's not supernatural at least,
However unexpected.

    CURATOR (*who has examined the crack carefully*).
                            That has come
Since yesterday. I brought two poets here.
They saw much, spoke much. What they chiefly saw
And spoke of was the parting of these lips.
A finger's breadth divides them; yet, they said,
That finger's breadth was infinite as time.

VISITOR (*indulgently*).

Poets are fanciful.

CURATOR

One even found
A likeness in it to the small sea-crack,
The Nelson-watched, untraversable line,
Which, parting Sicily from Naples, balked
Napoleon's scornful legions.

VISITOR (*rather bored*).

Poetry
Has uses doubtless. It is true the crack
Passes between the lips.

CURATOR

As if to place
A second bar between them. But the fact
Perplexes all inquiry. All was still,
No jar, no thunder-peal, nor more of wind
Than fans the cheek and fails to lift the hair.
We never move the urn.

VISITOR (*thoughtfully*).

The other day
In France they told me of a curious thing,
A picture in a second turning black.
No cause — a half-year's marvel. Afterwards
Men found the artist who had wrought the thing

Had in that very second stabbed a man,
While gaming in a tavern.

CURATOR

But the man
Who carved these figures died in Greece long since.
Two thousand years have ground his hardest bone
To powder.

VISITOR

It is true. (*Roger enters with the* "Times.")

ROGER (*to Curator*).

The paper, sir.

CURATOR

Oh, thank you. Roger, have you seen that crack?

ROGER

What crack, sir? (*His eye follows the Curator's
hand.*) The urn! The urn! Cracked! Sir, I swear
The thing was whole last night.

CURATOR

No doubt, no doubt.

ROGER (*clenching his fist*).

Some scoundrel!

VISITOR

Or that ancient felon Time.

CURATOR (*who has unfolded the* "Times").

We shall explore this further, be assured. (*Glances at paper*.)
Ah!

VISITOR

Some ill tidings?

CURATOR (*reading*).

"John Keats died in Rome
Yesterday at ten-thirty."

VISITOR (*politely*).

Who was he?

CURTAIN

TURNPIKES IN ARCADY

AUTHOR'S NOTE

Extract from Leonard Huxley's editorial comment on Elizabeth Barrett Browning's "Letters to her Sister," *Cornhill Magazine,* May, 1929.

"Wilson, the lady's maid, eventually became as Italianate as any dream of her poet-mistress, once she had got over her Puritan shock at the nudes in the picture galleries; and after being disappointed by a faithless Guardsman in the service of the Tuscan Grand Duke she made a very happy marriage with the Browning's manservant Ferdinando Romagnoli."

For further material on the "Guardsman" see *Cornhill Magazine,* August, 1929, pages 246–49. In this play the faithlessness has been excised, but, by way of indemnity to the Erinyes, the "Guardsman" is unhistorically represented as a stabber of Austrians and a fugitive from justice. "Righi" is the real surname; "Filippo" is the playwright's substitute for the unknown reality.

※※

From the *Letters of Robert Browning and Elizabeth Barrett Browning.*

"Mr. Kenyon (for I only quote where you may verify if you please) *he* says my commonsense strikes him, and its contrast with my muddy metaphysical poetry."—R. B.

"As to 'practical sense' I never saw, I confess, much to praise you for — but you began by making a great profession of it, please to remember."—E. B. B.

AUTHOR'S NOTE

"And talking of reasons, and reasonable people in general, I thought . . . after you went away on Wednesday, and I began to remember how you had commended your own common sense and mine — I thought that it might be very well for you to do it, inasmuch as nobody else would." — E. B. B.

"You have excellent practical sense after all and should exercise it." — E. B. B.

"Flush beats us both in common sense, dearest, we must acknowledge, let us praise each other for it ever so." — E. B. B.

TURNPIKES IN ARCADY

⋙⋙⋙⋙⋙ ⋙⫸⫷ ⫷⫷⫷⫷⫷⫷

CHARACTERS

ROBERT BROWNING

ELIZABETH BARRETT
BROWNING

WILSON, *Mrs. Browning's
maid*

FILIPPO RIGHI

*Place: Casa Guidi, Florence. Time: the spring of 1848.
The three scenes take place in the same room at twelve
o'clock noon, seven at night, and twelve midnight of the
same day.*

SCENE I

*The curtain rises on the Brownings' sitting room in Casa
Guidi. Large double windows (the " Casa Guidi Windows ") at rear center overlook a Florentine piazza.
Doors at left and right lead to bedroom and corridor.
Fireplace in upper right-hand corner; mantel with ornaments and two or three books. Table upstage left cov-
ered with books and papers. To left of center, not too
far from front, Mrs. Browning's sofa. Easy chair to right
of sofa; other chairs here and there. Except the table,
everything is distinctly, though informally, and, as it
were, unconcernedly, neat.*

*Elizabeth on the sofa; Flush, the dog, sleeping on the
sofa at her feet; Robert in the easy chair.*

ELIZABETH. I am sure, after all, that I am practical.

ROBERT. You shall be what you please, Ba. You shall be six feet tall, if you like.

ELIZABETH (*looking at her feet*). That would leave no room for Flush on the sofa — it would be unpractical. No, dearest, on the whole, I will not be six feet tall, unless you insist on it.

ROBERT. I? Not at all. You're easier to carry upstairs as you are.

ELIZABETH. Ah, those stairs! (*Remorsefully.*) *And I let you do it!*

ROBERT. There should have been three flights.

ELIZABETH. When you say foolish things like that, don't you see that you prove that I am quite right in — (*She pauses.*)

ROBERT. When did I deny that you were quite right in anything? What do you want to be quite right in now?

ELIZABETH. In saying that, in spite of appearances, (don't I know, dear, how the appearances are against me?) that I am essentially — temperamentally — practical — more so even than you? Ah, you needn't smile. You *mustn't* smile. I know how much I don't know. I've been brought up in a dark room. I don't know my way in Cheapside.

But if I had been brought up in Cheapside, I shouldn't have been run over. My instinct is to see the plain side when there *is* a plain side, and when there's light enough to see by.

ROBERT. Why see the plain side — you, a poet?

ELIZABETH (*smiling*). What are you?

ROBERT. A poet with a bond to the earth. A balloon with a parachute.

ELIZABETH. I don't see why a man should be more sensible than a woman.

ROBERT. So that the woman may be more poetic.

ELIZABETH (*thoughtfully*). But is anybody — man or woman — really more poetic for lacking common sense? I should think the greatest poet would be the first to see where the poetic would be out of keeping, just as the real lover would be the last man to prattle about his love in an omnibus. A true poet wouldn't eject the practical from its own place — its right place — any more — (*She is at a loss for an instant.*)

ROBERT. Any more than he would rhyme his prose.

ELIZABETH. Yes. It's quite indecent of you not to agree with me, Robert, when you say what I mean so much better than I do.

ROBERT. I do agree about the principle. What I quarrel with is the application.

ELIZABETH. To me?

ROBERT. Must I say so? Yes, then, to you.

ELIZABETH. Of course you *are* right in one way. I haven't the practical faculty; I lack the training. But I do think I have a practical bent. I don't like confusions, and one avoids confusions in one's own life by giving the humblest part all that belongs to it, just as one avoids confusions in the state by giving the humblest citizen all that belongs to him.

ROBERT. You should have no humblenesses in your life. Shall I tell you what they would be like there — intruders that they are? Like the English in Italy.

ELIZABETH. Italy views the English very practically.

ROBERT. I know they cheated us in Pisa.

ELIZABETH. I am very thankful to Pisa. It shows that even man is practically fallible.

ROBERT. In our honeymoon we believed in all the world — even in landlords.

ELIZABETH. We should have been just as good poets if we hadn't allowed them to cheat us. Think how shrewd we now are, and still we are writing verses.

ROBERT. You talk about avoiding confusions. Do you know where I found two stanzas of *Casa Guidi Windows* yesterday?

ELIZABETH. Not in the fireplace, did you?

ROBERT. No, no; on the back of a receipted bill.

ELIZABETH. Oh, you mustn't blame a poet's wife for that, dear. The stanzas were a pæan in honor of the fact that the bill had been receipted.

ROBERT. At all events the poet took a receipt. That was businesslike.

ELIZABETH. Was it businesslike to leave it around where a woman scribbler could appropriate it to her frivolities?

ROBERT. No, that wasn't business; that was inspiration.

ELIZABETH. I *am* untrained; I've only the bent, not the faculty. But poets and women, I will contend, are naturally as practical as bankers or men. Do you know one line in Shakespeare that I particularly like?

ROBERT. What line?

ELIZABETH. "At what o'clock tomorrow shall I send?"

ROBERT. The dullest line in Shakespeare, I should say.

ELIZABETH. Not at all. It is said by Juliet in the balcony scene. It is a practical line in the most romantic dialogue in literature, and the point is that it is uttered by a woman.

ROBERT. That is just what I was always saying in our letter writing; "At what o'clock tomorrow shall I send (or come)?"

ELIZABETH. Yes, I thought of nothing but days and hours in those times. My true vocation, Robert, was to be a railway clerk. I should have been dismayingly statistical, and should have made it a point to be very short with you when you, an unpractical man, couldn't find your way out of the time-tables.

ROBERT. Time-tables would perplex an accountant. It is irrational not to be perplexed by time-tables.

ELIZABETH. By that test you were rationality itself, dear, when you eloped with me.

ROBERT. That was a practical elopement; it succeeded.

ELIZABETH. Yes, but should I not have a tiny bit of credit for that? The difficulties were all in Wimpole Street.

ROBERT (*taking her hand*). From which Fate barred me — execrable Fate.

ELIZABETH. I know, beloved. But vanity will have
its foolish boast at last. Andromeda had to face
her dragon alone, or break the chain that bound
her to the rock, and fly from him. All her winged
Perseus could do was to hover in the air at a distance above her — so far above her, dearest. And
here we are after all in Casa Guidi. All of which
shows, I think, that Andromeda was very practical.

ROBERT. Ah, but Casa Guidi was not her place, but
the firmament, where the Greek astronomers put
her.

ELIZABETH (*in a low voice*). Not *alone* there, dearest — not alone.

ROBERT. I shall reward you for that by admitting that
you manage the woman's side of an elopement
very practically.

ELIZABETH. Ah, that is your magnanimity. Shall I
be maganimous, too? It was really Wilson that
did everything. I renounce the personal credit. It
is enough to vindicate my sex.

ROBERT. Domestics have to be sensible. If they
weren't — (*He completes the sentence by a gesture.*)

ELIZABETH. They couldn't make it up to us by their

verses — that is true. I don't expect people to be as practical as their domestics, Robert. But I don't see why the Tennysons and the Landors shouldn't be as practical as the Kenyons and the Forsters.

ROBERT. Write that to Forster and Kenyon.

ELIZABETH. No, that's one proof of my practicality — I don't write *that* to *them*.

ROBERT. Men of affairs do cling to the notion of an artist's incompetence. That's their breastwork.

ELIZABETH (*smiling*). Isn't that why you men cling to the notion of a woman's incompetence? That's your breastwork.

ROBERT. Am I to have no dyke against the flood of your superiorities?

ELIZABETH. You shall talk no more like that. (*Knock at door right.*) Come in. (*Wilson enters; a trim, wholesome English maid, very pleasant, yet very proper, in a black dress with the conventional reliefs.*) What is it, Wilson?

WILSON. The joiner has brought back your desk with the new drawers. Shall Filippo bring it in?

ELIZABETH (*at a loss*). Filippo?

WILSON. Filippo Righi, ma'am. He says he doesn't like to be called "Signor" when his coat is off.

ROBERT. The "Signor" is part of the uniform.

ELIZABETH. Isn't he on duty at the palace?

WILSON. No, the Grand Duke has let him off for the afternoon because he will be on duty tonight at the reception.

ELIZABETH. Very well. I shall feel quite ducal myself to be served by a servitor of the Grand Duke. (*Wilson, at door right, gives a tiny signal, and Filippo Righi, a tall guardsman in his shirt sleeves, enters with a small desk upon his shoulders. He is unable to make his guardsman's official bow, and smiles apologetically at the Brownings in recognition of the fact.*)

FILIPPO. Buon giorno.

ELIZABETH. Do you spend your holiday in carrying my furniture upstairs, Signor Righi?

FILIPPO (*in his struggling English*). For the Signora — and for Mees Weelson — I task myself joyfully.

ELIZABETH. Put down the desk, and we will find a place for it. (*Before obeying, the guardsman refers the point silently to Wilson. Wilson assenting, he puts down the desk. This by-play is enjoyed by Robert.*)

WILSON (*discreetly*). Where will you have the desk, ma'am?

ELIZABETH. In the old place, if you please, Wilson — at the left of the window, where it covers the frayed spot in the carpet. (*The guardsman looks at Wilson again, and again Robert smiles.*)

WILSON (*after a very brief, but appreciable — somewhat highly appreciable — pause*). You hear the Signora, Filippo.

ELIZABETH (*divining an arrière-pensée*). What is it, Wilson?

WILSON (*with great propriety*). Nothing, ma'am.

ROBERT. If you have a suggestion to make —

WILSON. I couldn't think of making any suggestion, sir — only, it occurred to me —

ELIZABETH. Tell us what occurred to you, Wilson.

WILSON. You see, in the hot afternoons we have to lower the left-hand shade, and there is not light enough for Mrs. Browning by the left-hand window. If Filippo were to put the desk under the right-hand window, there would be plenty of light. (*Moving upstage.*) We could put a footstool over the frayed spot in the carpet, and Flush could lie on the footstool when he wasn't lying on the manuscript. (*Flush, hearing his name, gets up and comes over to Wilson, expressing manifest disapproval of the frayed spot.*)

ROBERT. What do you think, Ba? The suggestion seems very practical.

ELIZABETH. Very. Is that why it didn't occur to us, Robert — either of us?

ROBERT. Very well, Filippo, do as Wilson says. They tell me that you are Filippo with your coat off.

FILIPPO (*now capable of a handsome bow, after putting down his burden*). Filippo — in any — any costume — for the Signor.

ELIZABETH. That is quite right. Thank you many times. It is really quite too much, Signor Righi, that you should have to lift that heavy desk.

WILSON (*with an air of modest proprietorship which does not escape the Brownings*). He is very strong. The desk is nothing to him. Come, Filippo. (*The guardsman smiles and bows with an embarrassment which is too Italian to be awkward. Then he follows Wilson out of the door right.*)

ELIZABETH. Wilson has certainly made a conquest.

ROBERT. In your Dumas *père* the guardsmen always appropriate the serving maids.

ELIZABETH (*smiling*). By way of a stepping-stone to their mistresses, Robert — don't forget that.

ROBERT. Filippo pauses on the stepping-stone.

ELIZABETH. It's a relief that Wilson is a sensible girl.

ROBERT. She was certainly right about the desk.

ELIZABETH. And I ought to know about desks—
surely we both ought.

ROBERT. Never mind. Some day we will combine
our practicalities and crush Wilson.

ELIZABETH. That wouldn't tell us which is really the
more practical. And till then I shall keep on saying that it is you who are the riotous romanticist.
You would have loved the beggar maid like
Cophetua. You *did* love her.

ROBERT (*denyingly*). When?

ELIZABETH. Beggars have no memory for dates. Any-
how your heroines are shamelessly romantic.
Don't you remember how in *Colombe's Birthday*
the duchess marries the advocate?

ROBERT. And in *Lady Geraldine's Courtship* how the
earl's daughter marries the poet?

ELIZABETH. I am romantic in my verse certainly.
One puts the flower into the vase. What I say—
or try to think—is that I don't put the flower
into the coal scuttle.

ROBERT. I wouldn't trust you not to drop flowers anywhere.

ELIZABETH. If a really practical occasion came up,
if it knocked at that door within the next few

minutes, (*she points right*) and if I knew enough about it to foresee results, I should be more just to the practical considerations than you would be. You smile, do you? That is a very vainglorious smile, and I shouldn't forgive it. But I will. You had a hundred reasons for laughing at me before. I am generous enough to let you have a hundred and one.

ROBERT. I shall blunder quite enough to satisfy you, I dare say. But I oughtn't to. I've been in the world sufficiently.

ELIZABETH. It wouldn't be want of power, dear, or lack of wisdom. But, while you were mustering your forces, some splendid great impulse would swoop down upon you like a falcon, and bear you up to its aerie. Naturally, having you, it wouldn't want me, and I should be left on the ground to deal practically with the groundlings.

ROBERT. Perhaps your falcon wouldn't take me.

ELIZABETH. Ah, that is where you are quite mistaken. *My* falcon would.

ROBERT. Being practical is being just to all the stupidities, and that is what you are too great to be.

ELIZABETH. Poor stupidities! Don't they need a little justice, too?

ROBERT. Yes, and here I am to see that they get it. You know the children of this world are wiser in their generation than the children of light.

ELIZABETH. As if that argument helped you!

ROBERT. I see nothing will convince you but experiment. Just wait.

ELIZABETH. *You* wait. (*Knock at the door.*)

ROBERT. Come in. (*Wilson enters with an air of importance which, like all other appurtenances to Wilson, is perfectly discreet.*)

WILSON. I wanted to speak to you, ma'am.

ELIZABETH. Certainly. What is it? (*Wilson flushes a little, but is silent.*) Do you want Mr. Browning to go away?

WILSON. I should be very glad if Mr. Browning would stay, ma'am. You see I need — I need some very practical advice. (*Elizabeth glances silently at Robert.*)

ELIZABETH. In that case he shall stay by all means. But you mustn't expect him to be too practical, Wilson. He's only a poet like myself.

WILSON (*doing the handsome thing*). No one would guess it from his actions, ma'am.

ROBERT (*crossing right and stopping before fireplace*). Take a chair, Wilson.

WILSON. Thank you, sir. I'd rather stand. (*She is now at right of center, facing Elizabeth.*) You see, ma'am — you see, Filippo wants to marry me.

ELIZABETH. My dear Wilson!

WILSON (*defensively*). I shouldn't have to leave you, ma'am — at least not for some time. Filippo has thought it all out. The landlord would let us have the flat below, and I could still be your maid. I made my wish on that point very clear to Filippo.

ROBERT. That is most generous and loyal on your part, Wilson, but here your own good must be your first concern — even our first concern. Do you *want* to marry him?

WILSON. Not without your approval, sir.

ROBERT. What do you want if we approve?

WILSON. He isn't easy to say "No" to, sir.

ELIZABETH. He certainly is very goodlooking, Wilson.

WILSON (*with dignified remoteness*). I am told that his looks are — passable.

ELIZABETH. But of course you mustn't make that your main object in a husband.

WILSON. I shouldn't, ma'am. I have been too close to a marriage that was founded on higher principles. (*This well-meant speech nearly shatters the gravity of both listeners.*)

ROBERT. What makes you think he has the higher principles?

WILSON. He's — he's very kind.

ROBERT. To you — for the instant. You should be shrewd enough to know, Wilson, that women in mating take a man's smooth ways as signs of character — or of disposition. Really they're signs only of his wishes.

WILSON (*meeting this bravely*). He's kind to other people besides me. When I was standing at the window yesterday, a goat upset the old woman's orange cart, and he helped her pick up all the oranges.

ROBERT. He knew you were at the window?

WILSON (*coloring with pleasure*). He always knows when I am at the window.

ROBERT. He would have to leave the Grand Duke's service if he married — you know that?

WILSON. His brother is a merchant in Florence. Filippo would go into business with him. He is tired of adventure.

ELIZABETH (*attentive*). Adventure?

WILSON. He was with Garibaldi for a month in the

South — before he took service with the Grand
Duke.

ELIZABETH AND ROBERT. With Garibaldi? (*Each is
abruptly made aware of his own lapse from practicality by the note of vivid exclamation in the
other's voice; each at once resumes allegiance to
the practical.*)

ELIZABETH. A month with Garibaldi pleads mightily
in his behalf, Wilson; neither Robert nor I would
grudge him honor for that. But where the induce-
ments are greatest we must be most watchful.
You must think, my dear girl — think very, very
seriously — that after all he is Italian and you
English.

ROBERT (*emulous of Elizabeth's self-control*). You
can't unlearn your past, Wilson — can't undo it —
he just as little.

ELIZABETH (*not to be outdone*). Italy and England
are very far apart, and it's a dangerous thing to
put the two of them on opposite sides of the same
dining table for a lifetime.

WILSON (*unresistingly*). Yes, ma'am.

ROBERT (*continuing the good work*). There's the
language, too.

WILSON. Filippo is teaching me Italian, and he's very quick with the English.

ROBERT. You could signal — flag each other — with words, Wilson, but you couldn't talk.

WILSON. Filippo's brother says that two languages are a good thing in marriage. When the man scolds, the wife never knows what he is saying, and that is so much the better.

ROBERT. Ah, but when the man scolds, the wife never knows what he is not saying, and that is so much the worse.

WILSON. Filippo would not scold me, perhaps. His manners are very good. I could not get the same manners in any Englishman who would marry me. (*This speech gives occasion for a quick glance between Elizabeth and Robert in which the truth of this, and the pathos of its truth, are mutually acknowledged.*)

ELIZABETH (*resuming the pursuit of duty*). Then there's the religion, Wilson.

WILSON (*with disquiet*). I know, ma'am. (*Hesitatingly.*) Filippo will let me do as I like. He says for him a Christian is just a Christian.

ROBERT. If a Christian were quite a Christian or just a Christian, which comes to much the same thing, that would be all very well. But, in fact, he's so much more, and, therefore, so much less.

ELIZABETH (*seeing that this is a little too Browningesque for Wilson*). Mr. Browning means, Wilson, that, when husband and wife go to the same place, they like to travel on the same train, and in the same compartment; and that that is true even when the journey is to the next world.

WILSON (*practically*). We should have a great deal to think of besides religion. (*But she is evidently disquieted.*)

ROBERT. The children, too — you have thought of them?

WILSON (*dropping her eyes*). No, sir.

ELIZABETH. They should be thought of most assuredly, Wilson. Suppose your boys went to mass, and your girls to chapel? Would that be desirable? And suppose the boys learned at mass that the Pope was God's vicar, and the girls learned at chapel that he was Antichrist?

WILSON (*faintly defensive*). They might all learn that way that the Pope didn't — didn't count.

ROBERT (*approvingly*). Good; but, you see, when the child finds out that half of what the priests say doesn't count, he asks next: "What about the other half?"

WILSON (*capitulating*). I see it wouldn't do, sir. You must be right, surely — since you are *both* so sure. A girl can't afford a mistake in a thing she can't change afterward. (*She comes to the sofa, and arranges the cushions for Elizabeth.*) But I *do* like Filippo, and he is as kind as any girl could wish — to children. (*Both the Brownings are distressed by this speech.*)

ELIZABETH (*in her most winning way*). We don't want to force your decision, Wilson — never for one moment. The question is far more yours than ours; you must decide, and decide freely. Only there is so much to be thought of, (*she draws Wilson's hand affectionately down through hers*) and what we want is to help you to think.

WILSON. You're very good, ma'am, and I've no doubt you're quite right. I don't want to be foolish, I'm sure. There's quite enough foolish girls in this world. (*In disposing of the last cushion she comes upon Flush, who has resumed his siesta at the end of the sofa. Wilson pauses to look at him, strokes him, and continues in a tone in which several emotions mingle.*) *He* likes Filippo.

ELIZABETH (*almost shamefacedly*). *We* all like him.

WILSON (*with a highly correct courtesy*). I thank you both. (*She goes out right. The Brownings look at each other, half amused and half distressed.*)

ROBERT (*coming to sofa*). Well, dear?

ELIZABETH (*looking up into his face*). We've done very well, Robert, haven't we? — very well, indeed. We were right, quite dreadfully right. Poor Wilson! But she shouldn't have yielded. That was really taking a most unfair advantage of us, Robert.

ROBERT (*taking Flush into his lap, as he resumes his seat in the easy chair*). One has qualms, dearest, inevitably, but one must be rational.

ELIZABETH. I listened to myself, and I couldn't help asking: "Who is this highly sensible person talking? It can't be Elizabeth Barrett. That poor creature is incapable of all this logic. It must be Mrs. Robert Browning." You were almost as formidable as I was, Robert. Not quite. When we go into business, I shall be the senior partner. Poor Wilson! No wonder she turned to Flush. Flush was the only romanticist left in this — this countinghouse.

ROBERT. Ba, Ba, Ba!

ELIZABETH. I know, dear. And you were perfectly right in telling Wilson what any lawyer or financier or tax assessor would have told her. When the pedestrians are on the right road, then the rider — even the rider on the winged horse, dearest — must follow their example. It doesn't matter if their shoes *are* dusty.

ROBERT. Her submission makes us wince — that can't be stopped. But look at the case fairly. Englishwoman — Protestant — servant wants to marry Italian — Catholic — guardsman. Risks had to be pointed out; we did nothing more.

ELIZABETH (*seriously*). I am quite of your mind, really. We have a special responsibility toward Wilson. It is through us that she is in Italy far away from her natural advisers and exposed to unusual temptations. We were bound to save her, if possible, from any evil consequences of such a step. Only —

ROBERT. Only —

ELIZABETH (*softly*). It is hard for a love like ours to put a ban upon any other love.

ROBERT. It's not *our* love that we take from Wilson.

ELIZABETH. Not ours, but something perhaps of the same relative magnitude in her smaller life.

ROBERT. But where the good is a chance? Marriage is a gaming table.

ELIZABETH. True, but if one has made a fortune at Monte Carlo one's self —

ROBERT. Preaching is graceless, then, I grant. But even so, isn't it necessary? Sense must come first.

ELIZABETH. It's so easy to be sensible when somebody else pays the bills. You and I are admirably sensible this morning, but Wilson pays the bills. Poor Wilson — the poor Filippo! Robert, shouldn't I lend Wilson my copy of *The Three Musketeers* — or buy her an English version? Dumas might teach her the immorality of guardsmen.

ROBERT. Dumas might instruct her in their fascinations.

ELIZABETH. That is a field, I fear, in which Wilson has no discoveries to make. Is it one o'clock yet?

ROBERT (*consulting his watch*). Ten minutes short.

ELIZABETH. I needn't hurry to dress, then. I'm glad this happened at noon.

ROBERT. Why?

ELIZABETH. The hour braced my practicality. When day is poised at its zenith, one yearns for equipoise. Nobody could part two lovers at twilight. The dusk would unman us.

ROBERT. Poets would find it hard.

ELIZABETH. Poets? But you and I, after this, are merely financiers. That reminds me. You didn't forget to fetch the ten-pound note to pay the landlord the rent tomorrow?

ROBERT. I have it.

ELIZABETH. That is good. I should have hated to have to pawn my locket to appease the landlord. (*Wilson appears in doorway left.*)

WILSON. It is time for you to dress, ma'am.

ELIZABETH (*very kindly*). Coming, Wilson. (*Wilson disappears.*) Oh, you *don't* have to carry me, Robert.

ROBERT. I *do* have to. I insist on having to. It makes the carrying seem so much more —

ELIZABETH (*smiling*). Practical? (*He nods, then takes her in his arms. Flush surveys the movement with a critical interest that passes finally into approval.*)

ROBERT. Wilson looked very pretty when she blushed.

ELIZABETH. Let us hope we shan't have to find out whether she looks ugly when she's pale.

CURTAIN

SCENE II

The same. Seven in the evening. Dusk. Elizabeth on the sofa, her face turned toward the window. Wilson enters right.

WILSON. Shall I draw the curtains, ma'am?

ELIZABETH. No, I am letting the night do that for me.

WILSON (*coming to sofa*). Is there anything else I can do?

ELIZABETH. Nothing, thank you, Wilson. (*But something in Wilson's voice has caught her attention.*) Stay a moment. Let me look at you. (*Wilson faces Elizabeth reluctantly.*) Is anything the matter?

WILSON. Nothing—important.

ELIZABETH. That means that something is the matter. Sit down here. (*She draws Wilson down upon the sofa.*) Is there anything new—about Filippo?

WILSON (*really concerned for her mistress*). I will tell you in the morning, ma'am.

ELIZABETH. Tell me now. I am very strong tonight, Wilson.

WILSON (*in two minds*). I'm sure I oughtn't to tell you, but—(*the kindness in Elizabeth's eyes is irresistible*) Filippo is hurt. (*Wilson in her sudden feeling is a girl again.*)

ELIZABETH (*one arm around Wilson*). Seriously?

WILSON. No. The hurt isn't serious.

ELIZABETH. What is serious, then? Can't you tell me the story plainly — just as it happened?

WILSON (*more calmly*). When I left you this noon, I told Filippo I should not marry him. He — he wasn't angry. He just looked at me out of those eyes of his.

ELIZABETH (*quietly*). I know their eyes.

WILSON. He went to a tavern — and drank. He was reckless, ma'am. (*She cannot quite hide her pride in the fact.*)

ELIZABETH. And he quarreled with someone in the tavern?

WILSON. Filippo stabbed the other man in the right breast.

ELIZABETH (*in a low voice*). Fatally?

WILSON. Filippo thinks it was only a flesh wound. He doesn't quite know. The doctor came with the police, and Filippo ran away before they came.

ELIZABETH (*after a moment's thought*). If the man's hurt is only a flesh wound, I don't think there'll be any lastingly serious consequences. The Italians are hasty with weapons. Italian judges know that, and are lenient accordingly.

WILSON. But there's another thing, ma'am. The man Filippo stabbed was an Austrian.

ELIZABETH (*gravely*). That is rather serious. The Grand Duke is an Austrian, you know, Wilson.

WILSON. I know. (*With some difficulty.*) He wasn't just an ordinary Austrian.

ELIZABETH (*quickly, but kindly*). What kind of Austrian was he?

WILSON. He was a coachman at the Austrian embassy.

ELIZABETH (*again putting her arm around Wilson*). That is very serious indeed, Wilson. I don't know whether you know that in such a country as Italy, and indeed almost anywhere, embassies are almost more sacred than cathedrals. I think poor Filippo would have been wiser to stab a bishop.

WILSON. You think it very wrong, then?

ELIZABETH. Wrong? I? I wish I were Filippo's judge, or Robert! But an Austrian Italy has other standards. Filippo should not lose an hour in leaving Florence, Wilson.

WILSON. They will watch every train and stop every carriage. The only way is to send Filippo at midnight by barge down the Arno. Then he can take ship at Leghorn for the South. He has friends there — people who love Garibaldi.

ELIZABETH. They will help him, doubtless.

WILSON. Yes. You see the quarrel was about Garibaldi. The Austrian called Garibaldi a vile name, and then Filippo —

ELIZABETH (*rising and pacing the room, her eyes on fire*). He stabbed an Austrian for insulting Garibaldi! (*Turning, she faces Wilson.*) He is a man fit to be loved, Wilson. He is a man one could follow through the world.

WILSON (*cautiously*). Do you — quite — mean that?

ELIZABETH. Do I mean what?

WILSON. Filippo wants me — to go with him — tonight.

ELIZABETH. To float down the Arno — in a barge — at midnight — with the man one loved — to the sea — the sea and Garibaldi! What an anticipation! What an experience! What a memory!

WILSON (*half frightened, half spellbound*). You would approve of my going, ma'am?

ELIZABETH (*admonished by the word "approve"*). Approve! Approve! No, no, I might understand, I might sympathize, I might admire, dearest Wil-

son, but approve — no, no, the step would be very
rash. I am sure Mr. Browning would think it
rash.

WILSON. I thought Mr. Browning would think that.

ELIZABETH (*piqued*). Didn't you think *I* would think
that?

WILSON. I thought you would both think it. I am
always sure that two people so wise and good as
you couldn't both be wrong at once.

ELIZABETH (*touched*). Thank you, Wilson. I am
wise, you see, because I never differ from my husband. And Mr. Browning and I should both
strongly disapprove of your setting out on so rash
an expedition — in such unheard-of circumstances.
We might envy you, Wilson — I mean I, being a
foolish, romantic woman, might envy you, but I
should disapprove.

WILSON (*clinging to common sense*). I don't think
we could go anyway, ma'am. Filippo couldn't pay
the fare for two.

ELIZABETH (*quickly*). That is unlucky. I mean that
is very fortunate. (*She reflects.*) I happen to be out
of money just now, and of course in such a matter
it would be impossible to apply to Mr. Brown-

ing — to say nothing of my own strong disapproval of the step. (*More reflection.*)

WILSON. I couldn't take money from you for that,
ma'am.

ELIZABETH (*who has been running her hand up and
down the chain of the locket that she wears*).
Wilson, you must make your own decision. Be
rash if you must. Be wise if you can. But you
must not allow the having or not having of a few
pounds, shillings, and pence to snatch the decision
from you. Take this locket. It was my grandmother's. It is worth at least five pounds. Because
she was a brave woman I value it and her. Do not
hesitate to take it. It is not money, it is choice and
freedom that I put into your hands. (*Elizabeth,
passing the chain once more through her fingers
as if in lingering valediction, presses it into Wilson's vainly deprecating hands; then, as if to end
the protests, she moves toward the windows. She
speaks, half to herself, half to Wilson.*) The brave
Filippo! As if a nation that bred hearts like that
could be ground irretrievably under any despot's
heel! The moon is coming up. After midday has
dinned into our ears the insanity of all high ad-

venture, the moon rises to justify us. As if all the brave, foolish young hearts that died to no purpose had bequeathed each its single ray to the brightness of the orb, and its splendor had become an urgence for us to be brave and foolish to the end of time! (*She turns back to Wilson, her face aglow.*)

WILSON. If I went, ma'am, I should have to go at twelve o'clock tonight. A closed carriage is coming for Filippo.

ELIZABETH. Is Filippo in this house?

WILSON. No, in the basement opposite. That is where Nunziata lives, the girl who will come to you to take my place if—if I go.

ELIZABETH. Nunziata is a good girl, but I shall miss you very much.

WILSON. Shouldn't I speak to Mr. Browning about this?

ELIZABETH (*disconcerted*). Mr. Browning? (*She takes two or three steps in evident uncertainty, then, at center, faces Wilson.*) Mr. Browning has a practical mind, as you know, Wilson. He would feel very strongly the practical objections to the plan you have in mind. I feel those objections very powerfully myself. That is why I have refused to give you my approval.

WILSON (*shrewdly*). Perhaps that's a reason why I should speak to him, ma'am.

ELIZABETH (*very kindly*). It is your own secret, Wilson. Do quite as you like. At the same time if you should make up your mind to the great step (*her eyes involuntarily kindle*) it might be well to be as little talkative as possible.

WILSON (*hesitatingly*). Shall you tell it to Mr. Browning, ma'am?

ELIZABETH. I? Certainly. There are no secrets between *us*. You should know that, Wilson. I shall tell Mr. Browning everything — (*with an effect of incidentality*) in the morning. (*The eyes of the two women meet in a look in which mutual understanding is combined on Wilson's part with not a little personal bewilderment.*) Will Filippo's face be permanently scarred?

WILSON. The doctor didn't think so.

ELIZABETH. If the scars did last, what matter? They would sanctify the woman's lips that touched them. (*She goes to the window for a last look, then turns back.*) I should like to sit up — to stand up—all night, and watch. But that would not do. I should be questioned. (*She pauses with the compunction of a wife concealing something for the first time from her husband.*) I cannot sleep, Wilson, but I will undress and lie down, and you shall bring me a lamp and the copy of Leopardi — you know that?

WILSON. The one with the binding half off? Yes, ma'am, I'll fetch it. (*She fetches the book from one of the cases, and goes out left with Elizabeth. A few seconds elapse before the door right opens softly, and Robert enters with a swift but noiseless step. He is followed by a man muffled in a cloak which on removal discloses what bruises and bandages have left of the handsome features of Filippo Righi. His shoulder is carried in a sling.*)

ROBERT (*imperative, but friendly*). Come in. Keep from the window. *I'll* look out. (*Goes to window, looks out, returns, speaks very low.*) All is right. No police in the square. You can go back in five minutes. Sit down. (*Goes to door left, listens, and returns.*) Mrs. Browning, by good luck, is asleep. (*Robert lights a candle, and the two men seat themselves in armchairs right.*) I must hear more, but we must not speak loud. All sorts of misfortunes might follow. You might be nabbed by the police. It might even wake Mrs. Browning.

FILIPPO. Mrs. Browning — would not like me — in the house?

ROBERT. She would sympathize with you only too much. She must be guarded from herself.

FILIPPO (*simply*). She is a great lady.

ROBERT. What did you stab him with?

FILIPPO. A dagger, Signor. Wait. I will show you. (*Shows dagger to Robert.*)

ROBERT (*taking it eagerly*). That is *the* dagger. You shouldn't carry that around.

FILIPPO. I need him chiefly now, Signor.

ROBERT (*pointing to a stain*). That is Austrian blood?

FILIPPO. Yes, that is the — the enamel on Italian daggers.

ROBERT (*turning the weapon in his hand*). To picture it! Italy should hoard these daggers, chase them in gold, and hang them in her churches. You stabbed him in the right breast?

FILIPPO (*apologetically*). I could not reach the left.

ROBERT. Which drew first?

FILIPPO. He, Signor, with the rapier. But before that

I strike him with the fist. When he called Garibaldi " schmutziges Tier."

ROBERT. You know German?

FILIPPO. Only the ugly words. The Austrians teach us those.

ROBERT (*between his teeth*). Hounds! (*He gets up.*) Filippo, show me. Where were you, and where was he?

FILIPPO (*getting up*). I sit here, Signor. (*Points to chair at stage right.*) I drink beer. You shall be Austrian (*he comes to table*) — you sit at table, you drink Chianti. (*Robert sits at table, and Filippo in the chair he has just indicated.*) You drink Chianti with two friends, you laugh, you talk German, you call Garibaldi " schmutziges Tier." I sit, I drink, I think of Mees Weelson, and on a sudden I hear you do that — that savageness to Garibaldi. I am by in a second, you are on your feet, (*both men suit the action to the words*) I give you — I give you — that. (*He mimics the act of striking.*)

ROBERT (*gleefully*). Bravo! (*But he is rubbing the left side of his head.*)

FILIPPO. The table shake, and the glasses fall. (*He demonstrates with unintended loudness.*)

ROBERT. Sh— Sh! The Signora!

FILIPPO (*much abashed*). Perdoni, Signor.

ROBERT. Wilson wants to go with you on this trip tonight, Filippo?

FILIPPO. She say not "Yes," not "No." She say "Wait."

ROBERT. Wilson can't rough it, you know. She's always sat on cushions — the edge of her mistress' cushions.

FILIPPO. My wife should not — how do you say? — rough it. I have kinsmen in Sorrento.

ROBERT. And the Signora?

FILIPPO. Nunziata will take Mees Weelson's place.

ROBERT (*after meditation*). I ought to tell you that this project is delirium. Another man would. My wife would. (*He glances guiltily toward the door left, then heartens himself by a glance at the moon through the window.*) If that rising disc were the sun's, I would, too. (*He rises, and walks musingly.*) An English lady's maid! A guardsman's wife in Florence! *Just* conceivable. A trooper's wife in Southern Italy. Even I, Robert Browning, whose diet is extravagance, balk at that. (*He takes another step, and pauses.*) Why, after all, am I Robert Browning, and not — say, Sir Robert

Peel? Shall I preach caution to generous impulse, I whose patent from Nature is to urge rashness upon despicable caution? (*He has almost forgotten Filippo, and has altogether forgotten the limits of Filippo's competence in English.*) An English lady's maid! But if she *wished* it? If the wish were its own sanction. Wilson equal to the resolve — a miracle to start with! Equal to the fulfilment — that is only miracle number two. If one shoulders an Apennine, why not an Alp? (*On the last few words his voice rises to its normal masculine vigor.*)

FILIPPO (*alarmed*). Signor, Signor — the Signora!

ROBERT. Miscreant that I am! Thank you, Filippo. (*He sits down.*) If I dared but wake her to advise you! — she whose mind is so pellucid in its very ardors, in whom the wind of the spirit moves only to *blow away* the mists from the intelligence!

FILIPPO. You think I should go without Mess Weelson, Signor?

ROBERT. I cannot advise now. At this moment I should give you very bad advice indeed. The world has shrunk for me to a barge floating down moon-blanched Arno at midnight, and a woman's hand locked in her proscribed and fleeing lover's.

FILIPPO (*with admiration*). You should have been an Italian, Signor.

ROBERT. I should indeed. I should be now at Garibaldi's side, and *she* with *me*. (*Taking fire at the thought.*) Filippo, if Wilson will go with you, *take* her. If the gods are poets enough to love madmen, they will watch over you.

FILIPPO. You approve, then, Signor?

ROBERT. Approve? I tell you that the step is madness. Have you money enough for two, Filippo?

FILIPPO. Not for two.

ROBERT (*reflectively*). Wilson must be shielded. The first hardships cut deepest — count most. Ease for a companion means ease for self; the expense is more than doubled. (*He extracts a ten-pound note from his purse, poises it hesitatingly between his fingers, looks misgivingly toward the door left.*) After all, who minds a yelping landlord? Let curs howl — only not outside her window.

FILIPPO. No, Signor, *please* — no money.

ROBERT. Filippo, Wilson must decide for herself. But if she decides on other grounds to be fearless, she must not be kept from her purpose by the miserable exactions of tollmen and innkeepers. Take this ten pounds — no refusals! (*He forces the note upon Filippo.*)

FILIPPO. Many thanks, Signor. (*Wilson enters left. Seeing the two men, she pauses, closing the door behind her.*)

ROBERT (*in a low voice*). Come in, Wilson. Is Mrs. Browning asleep?

WILSON (*now at center*). No, sir. She has been reading Le — Leopardi.

ROBERT. Leopardi is no sedative. I must take away the book. You and Filippo have much to say to each other. Say it, if you can, across the street. Goodnight. (*He goes out left.*)

FILIPPO (*rising and taking Wilson's hand*). He is very good, Weelson. She is good, too. Is that the way all the English love?

WILSON (*with great emphasis*). No, that's the way *they* love.

FILIPPO. The Italians are passionate, (*he presses Wilson's hand*) and the English are constant; but *they* — they are passionate and constant, too. (*They move right.*) Is it true that they ran away together?

WILSON (*reprovingly*). They were married *a whole week* before they ran away.

FILIPPO. I would have married you a week ago, Weelson.

WILSON. That's very different. You see Mr. Browning doesn't stab people. (*They go out right, arm-in-arm.*)

CURTAIN

SCENE III

The same. Midnight. Bright moonlight on the rear windows. Elizabeth, with shawl over nightdress, steals out of the room left, and glides to a station at left of the windows overlooking the square. Wrapping herself in a curtain fold, she looks out. Shortly after, Robert, in trousers and jacket, issues from the same room, and, gliding noiselessly to a position at right of window, looks down into the square.

ELIZABETH (*hearing a sound*). Robert!

ROBERT (*equally amazed*). Ba! (*They gaze stupefied at each other.*)

ELIZABETH. You here!

ROBERT. But you, dearest, but you!

ELIZABETH. You weren't—weren't looking for Wilson?

ROBERT. Then *you* knew?

ELIZABETH (*all compunction*). Dearest, how could I *not* tell you?

ROBERT (*remorsefully*). How much did *I* tell *you?* I am a trickster, dear. After this you shall call me Metternich.

ELIZABETH. Will you call me Talleyrand? You must

really throw me into the Arno, Robert. It is only at the bottom of the Arno that I shall get back the least particle of my self-respect.

ROBERT. Did Wilson tell you?

ELIZABETH. Yes. And you — Filippo told you?

ROBERT. Yes. (*Piteously.*) You had gone to bed.

ELIZABETH. But you came in and spoke to me. You took from me my Leopardi.

ROBERT. And you told me nothing about Wilson.

ELIZABETH. How could I tell you, dear? You had been so terribly practical at noon.

ROBERT. As if the sands in the hourglass stopped running at noonday!

ELIZABETH. No, they run and run, and they turn to pearl under the moon.

ROBERT. Moonlight evokes the sprites. One of them coaxed me to deceive you.

ELIZABETH. We are too much alike, Robert, to be able to deceive each other. It's like trying to hide a pimple from one's image in the glass.

ROBERT. Are we so much alike? Can you tell me what I am thinking of now?

ELIZABETH. The square? Wilson? (*He nods, and they turn, smiling, toward the windows.*)

ROBERT. There is the carriage—across the street—
out of the moonlight.

ELIZABETH. Is the coachman on the box? I can't see.

ROBERT. Yes. The carriage door is open. Filippo is
expected.

ELIZABETH. Filippo will come from this side.

ROBERT. Why?

ELIZABETH. He will be fetching Wilson—or parting
from her.

ROBERT. She may stay after all—poor girl.

ELIZABETH. Or go—poor girl.

ROBERT. There are so many poverties.

ELIZABETH (*with fire*). Robert, shall we go down
now to talk to Wilson—

ROBERT. To see that she goes—or that she doesn't?

ELIZABETH (*capitulating with a smile*). We might
decide on the stairway.

ROBERT (*looking out*). There is Filippo.

ELIZABETH (*quivering*). Alone? (*She looks out.*)

ROBERT (*with circumspect gentleness*). Alone. (*They
look at each other in a common endeavor to
disown a common disappointment.*)

ELIZABETH. Filippo's good sense was always trust-
worthy. (*She sighs.*)

ROBERT. Our anxiety was thrown away. (*He gnaws his lip.*)

ELIZABETH (*looking out*). *Was* it thrown away? Look, look, Robert. Who is that crossing the square?

ROBERT. It is — it *is* Wilson. (*Their eyes turn to each other to express their common dismay, then withdraw hastily in chagrin at having expressed a quite different feeling.*)

ELIZABETH. She won't really get into the carriage. She will turn back.

ROBERT (*not without excitement*). She is at the door, Ba — on the step. *She is inside.* (*Their hands meet, against their consciences, in a long, joyous clasp.*)

ELIZABETH. The door is closing.

ROBERT. They have driven off.

ELIZABETH. And a simple girl dared that. It is an act for Madame Roland. (*She turns from the window.*)

ROBERT (*following her*). To bed now, dearest. No more pilferings from the night.

ELIZABETH (*pleadingly*). Not yet. Not just yet. My sleep would be riddled with hoof beats. Light the lamp, Robert, and sit with me a little. (*He obeys.*)

No, I don't want the sofa. Fetch a chair, and we will sit together. (*They sit at midstage center.*) Robert, we're responsible for this.

ROBERT. I — not you.

ELIZABETH. Don't sleek things over for me, dear. I *did* tell Wilson that I disapproved of this elopement, but my disapproval was as transparent as a railway porter's unwillingness to take a double fee.

ROBERT. You should have heard me with Filippo.

ELIZABETH (*pleased*). Were you really quite outrageous with him, Robert?

ROBERT. Quite.

ELIZABETH. I haven't repented yet. There's too much moonlight. But what shall we think of this at twelve o'clock tomorrow? When that grand inquisitor, the midday sun, gets after us, where shall we be?

ROBERT. On the rack doubtless.

ELIZABETH (*laughing*). I shall recant — I feel I shall recant — unless somebody can persuade the earth to stop turning. What was it made us so sensible this morning?

ROBERT. I guess — dimly. Ba, why this morning did we snatch Wilson from Filippo, then not a fugitive from justice, but a highly respectable Filippo, bodyguardsman to the Grand Duke? Not because the idea wasn't practical enough. It wasn't romantic enough, Ba — that was *our* difficulty.

ELIZABETH (*dismayed, but amused*). You're right, you're dreadfully right. And just as soon as the idea became positively insane, something that Lydia Languish herself would have called ridiculous, we gave way — both of us.

ROBERT. I thought we both talked very practically to Wilson at noon. One of us, I know, did.

ELIZABETH. Yes, dear, we were both tremendous. Only, you see, with us, the practical was only a game, a test of ability, like a try at Latin verses. As soon as we'd filled out the last spondee, we relapsed into the comforting vernacular.

ROBERT. Shall we talk our own tongue henceforth — the romance tongue?

ELIZABETH. In this drench of moonlight what can one say to that but "Yes"? Only — (*She stops.*)

ROBERT (*divining her trouble*). Ba, don't blame yourself. You didn't approve.

ELIZABETH. My dear, I disapproved enticingly. It was Mark Antony discouraging the Roman populace from riot.

ROBERT. If error, it was yours and mine together.

Shouldn't I be proud to err with you? Isn't it strange how our very infirmities, when they become ties, become stays?

ELIZABETH. Infirmities, yes; but not guilts. If anything happened to Wilson, Robert—

ROBERT. Nothing *shall* happen.

ELIZABETH. Shall not? Ah, dear, can even you intimidate the Fates? Robert, we have bound poor Wilson to the stake of our romanticism, ready for Destiny to apply the torch. If it does, I shall bear the ashes of that burning upon my head forever.

ROBERT. She will be safe in Sorrento—with Filippo's people.

ELIZABETH. Who knows how safe *they* are? I fear for Wilson—(*Knock at door right.*) Who can that be—at this hour?

ROBERT. Go to your room, Ba. I will answer it. (*Elizabeth goes to door of room left, but remains standing on the threshold to await results. Robert opens door right.*)

WILSON (*offstage*). May I come in?

ROBERT (*thunderstruck*). Wilson!

ELIZABETH (*meeting Wilson in midstage*). Wilson! (*She takes the surprised Wilson into her arms and kisses her.*)

WILSON. Thank you, ma'am.

ROBERT (*at center again*). Then you *didn't* go, Wilson?

WILSON. Go? Oh, no, sir. I just said goodbye to Filippo.

ELIZABETH (*releasing her*). But we saw you, Wilson — we saw you get into the carriage. (*Wilson by this time has placed her mistress on the sofa; Robert takes an easy chair.*)

WILSON. That was to give Filippo the salve. I forgot the salve when we said goodbye.

ELIZABETH. The salve?

WILSON. I had a salve for his wound — and a spray. I had to show Filippo how to work the spray, and so I got into the carriage. They were late, you see.

ELIZABETH. And they set you down afterwards?

WILSON (*apologetically*). It was only two blocks. I hurried, and nobody spoke to me.

ROBERT. Then you wouldn't go with him?

WILSON. No. We talked it over, and we — well, we didn't think it was exactly — wise. (*Wilson's tone betrays a modest pride in this adjective.*)

ROBERT (*with a sigh of relief*). You were quite right.

WILSON. Yes, sir, I remembered what you and Mrs. Browning said at noon.

ELIZABETH. But this evening we said other things —
quite other things, Wilson. I mean I did.

WILSON. I know you said a little different this evening, but Filippo and I talked it over, and we
agreed that we'd better mind what you said
when — when you were more yourselves like.
(*The culprits exchange a look of rueful amusement.*)

ELIZABETH. Filippo was generous not to urge you.

WILSON. Filippo is very sensible, ma'am, except of
course when people call Garibaldi names. He told
me all about those places — mostly dirt and bandits and volcanoes. Being an English girl, I'm not
fond of dirt or volcanoes, and I'm sure I should
never get used to bandits, though Filippo says
there are some very honest fellows among them.

ROBERT. It's not our honesty, Wilson.

WILSON (*shyly*). There was another thing. If anything should happen to me down there, I couldn't
have my mistress blaming herself perhaps for —
for letting me half think that it was a fine thing
to be a friend to Garibaldi. I didn't want that to
come about. Besides, Nunziata, though she's a
very good girl in some respects — I don't deny it —
is very careless about the smelling salts.

ELIZABETH. I am very glad, Wilson, not to change you for the best of Nunziatas.

WILSON. I shall be ready in the morning. Goodnight, ma'am. Goodnight, sir.

ROBERT AND ELIZABETH. Goodnight, Wilson.

WILSON (*stopping as she moves right*). I forgot what I came for. (*Returning to Elizabeth.*) There's your grandmother's locket, ma'am. I thought you'd sleep more quietly if you knew it was in the room with you. (*Gives locket.*)

ROBERT (*confounded*). Elizabeth! You gave away your grandmother's locket! You cared to that degree!

ELIZABETH (*overwhelmed*). Dearest, what shall I say to you, and what won't you say to me? Have I convinced you at last that I am an imbecile? You know it now. I never saw a man who resisted so much testimony.

WILSON (*turning to Robert*). And here's the ten-pound note that you gave Filippo, sir, for my expenses. Filippo rather wanted to keep the ten-pound note, but when I explained to him that tomorrow was rent day, he saw at once that it was right to send it back.

ELIZABETH (*gasping*). The ten-pound note! The rent money! Robert!

ROBERT (*groveling*). I had nothing else.

ELIZABETH. Robert! Robert!

ROBERT. You see, dear, whom — I mean what — you married.

WILSON. It was very generous in Mr. Browning, and Filippo and I will always thank him, but perhaps it wasn't altogether practical. (*Enlighteningly.*) Landlords can be very disagreeable when they don't get their money. (*Elizabeth and Robert exchange a glance in which amusement mingles with discomfiture.*)

ROBERT (*gravely*). It is true that landlords need careful handling.

WILSON (*delighted with her pupil's aptness*). That's what I told Filippo, sir. Goodnight.

ELIZABETH. Goodnight, Wilson, I'm sure Mr. Browning's much obliged for the ten-pound note.

ROBERT. And Mrs. Browning for the locket. Goodnight. (*Wilson goes out right.*)

ELIZABETH (*with a sigh that is half a laugh*). Wilson is prodigious.

ROBERT. She inspires awe.

ELIZABETH. She ought to be treasurer to Garibaldi.

ROBERT. Which is like being *couturière* to Eve.

ELIZABETH. We are two babes in the wood, Robert, but after this we shall be safe — with Wilson. But why is she more practical than we? We could state the case for practicality better than she could. We could see the point more clearly. Only —

ROBERT. Only Wilson stuck to the fact she saw — that *is* practicality.

ELIZABETH. Wilson couldn't have thought of that.

ROBERT. *Wilson* needn't.

ELIZABETH. Let me see that ten-pound note. (*Robert gives it to her. She smooths it out between her fingers.*) How stupid a ten-pound note looks when one's going to pay rent with it! (*She continues to inspect the note.*) Shouldn't you like *me* to keep it for you till the morning?

ROBERT (*his laugh replying to hers*). Would you put it under your pillow — *with the locket?*

ELIZABETH (*returning the note*). I think I would.

ROBERT. Whatever you put under the pillow, you must put your head upon it — and at once.

ELIZABETH. I can't sleep. (*But she moves obediently toward door left.*)

ROBERT. I'll read you to sleep — when I've drawn these curtains. (*He draws curtains.*)

ELIZABETH (*offstage*). Robert!

ROBERT. Yes?

ELIZABETH (*drowsily*). Did you ever want to stab an Austrian?

ROBERT. Often, dear. I'll go and stab one now, if it'll help you to get to sleep quicker.

CURTAIN

EMPURPLED MOORS

AUTHOR'S NOTE

Branwell Brontë was tutor, Anne Brontë was governess, in the house of the Reverend Edmund Robinson of Thorp Center. The abrupt dismissal of Branwell and the sudden resignation of Anne have provoked much curiosity and speculation. Branwell professed to be in love with Mrs. Robinson. The theory of Mrs. Robinson's guilt, first advanced, and afterwards retracted and suppressed, by Mrs. Gaskell is losing currency and probability in our time. The present play adopts the kindlier view and makes the whole Robinson matter incidental to the evocation of an unverified but vivid possibility in the characters of the three sisters. Anne's vigil on the rug and Mrs. Robinson's visit to Haworth are pure invention.

EMPURPLED MOORS

➳➳➳-➳➳➳-➳➳➳-➳➳➳-➳➳ ➳➳)⟨⟨⟨ ⟨⟨⟨-⟨⟨⟨-⟨⟨⟨-⟨⟨⟨-⟨⟨⟨

CHARACTERS

PATRICK BRONTË, *perpetual curate of Haworth, York-shire, sixty-eight years old*

CHARLOTTE BRONTË, *twenty-nine years old*

PATRICK BRANWELL BRONTË, *twenty-eight years old*

EMILY BRONTË, *twenty-seven years old*

ANNE BRONTË, *twenty-five years old*

EVELYN ROBINSON

TABITHA ("TABBY"), *a domestic*

Time and place: Living room of Haworth Parsonage, nine o'clock of a summer evening in the year 1845.

Scene: a large, neatly kept, not incommodious, but rather somber living room. Furniture and carpet of good quality, but worn. At rear center, door leading to the parsonage garden, which adjoins the graveyard. In the rear wall two windows, one in right-hand corner. At the upper left-hand corner of the stage three steps rise to the obliquely set door of Mr. Brontë's study. In left wall two doors: the upper leads to Branwell's room; the lower to a passage. In the right wall down stage is a door lead-ing to parlor and to front of house. Farther back in the same wall a window. Sofa at right, and fireplace and mantelpiece at left, face each other down stage. Clock on mantelpiece. Between parlor door and window a bookcase. Beneath the bookcase, a desk and writing table with drawer. At right center, large work table with lighted lamp. Candles on the mantelpiece. Chairs and footstools.

As the curtain rises Charlotte and Anne enter from the parlor. Charlotte leads Anne to easy chair, left center, makes her comfortable, and stands erect with one hand laid firmly but affectionately on Anne's left shoulder.

ANNE. I didn't tell Emily quite everything, Charlotte.

CHARLOTTE. There's always a last, little thing that one doesn't tell Emily. I've found that out myself.

ANNE. Emily understands a great deal.

CHARLOTTE. A very great deal. But — (*she makes an emphatic gesture*) — when her understanding stops, it stops altogether.

ANNE (*abstractedly*). Yes.

CHARLOTTE. What one doesn't tell Emily is always the most interesting thing. You shall tell that to me now.

ANNE (*with effort*). It's not so *very* easy to tell you.

CHARLOTTE (*seating herself at Anne's right*). To-morrow, then.

ANNE (*trembling, but resolute*). I *daren't* put it off.

CHARLOTTE (*gravely kind*). Tell me now, then.

ANNE. When I found the note from Mrs. Robinson in Branwell's pocket — you understand, don't you, Charlotte, that he *asked* me to mend the coat, and that there wasn't any envelope? —

CHARLOTTE (*comfortingly*). I should have read it, anyway.

ANNE (*dubious, but cheered*). Should you? Well, when I read the note, and it *seemed* to say that Mrs. Robinson expected Branwell that night — that Thursday night when Mr. Robinson was away — at first I could think of nothing to do. Then suddenly at night — at eleven oclock — in my bed — a thought came to me. I got up and put on my clothes, and wrapped myself in a shawl. Then I climbed the stair to her door. There was a rug in front of it. I lay down on the rug, Charlotte. I wanted to see if — if anybody would come out of that door in the very early morning. (*Her voice sinks.*)

CHARLOTTE. That was a strange thing to do, Anne.

ANNE. Yes, it was strange. I knew it was strange. But I thought it was natural. You see, Charlotte, I had to *know*.

CHARLOTTE (*avoiding the crucial question*). You stayed there all night?

ANNE. Till the servants began to stir — yes.

CHARLOTTE (*still skirmishing*). Weren't you cold?

ANNE. Not very. The shawl was cashmere.

CHARLOTTE. And — and — nobody came out of the room?

ANNE (*looking into Charlotte's eyes*). Nobody. (*A silence.*)

CHARLOTTE (*suddenly*). Anne, tell me, were you *glad* when nobody came?

ANNE (*quickly*). Why shouldn't I be glad? Of course I was glad. (*She turns her eyes from Charlotte.*)

CHARLOTTE (*looking steadily in front of her*). You might have felt that the night was wasted.

ANNE. Wasted? That is a very odd word to use. Hadn't I found out?

CHARLOTTE (*in her usual voice*). Of course, of course. And that was all — all that you didn't tell Emily?

ANNE. Not quite. You see I had the note with me on the rug. It was folded in a glove in my bodice. The housemaid found the glove on the rug the next morning, and took it to Mr. Robinson. He came back early that forenoon.

CHARLOTTE. Well?

ANNE. He said: "Miss Brontë, here is a glove, and a letter in my wife's handwriting. I have not read the letter. I return the letter and the glove to you. Will you now permit me to read the letter?"

CHARLOTTE (*warmly*). He is a gentleman, Anne.

ANNE. Yes. That made it so hard.

CHARLOTTE. You didn't let him see the letter?

ANNE. No. The letter would have been all right if I could have told him about the night on the rug. But I couldn't. I couldn't let a man know what — what I must have been thinking on that rug.

CHARLOTTE (*with interest*). Did you think so much?

ANNE (*troubled*). No — not so very much. It was mostly — waiting.

CHARLOTTE. And then?

ANNE. Mr. Robinson dismissed Branwell that afternoon, and the next morning — I mean this morning — I came away.

CHARLOTTE. What kind of woman is she?

ANNE. Mrs. Robinson? She has a very good presence. She is stately and tranquil. That is the best of her. But she isn't ill-natured.

CHARLOTTE. The sort of woman to whom passion is worth about half as much as social standing?

ANNE. Yes, that is Mrs. Robinson. (*Tabby enters right, comes forward, and offers a card to Anne.*)

TABBY. Lady to see you, Miss Anne.

ANNE (*shrinking*). At this hour? I can see no one, Tabby.

CHARLOTTE. Let me see the card, Tabby. (*Tabby complies. Charlotte reads, and becomes thoughtful. Pause.*) I think you had better look at this card, Anne.

ANNE (*taking the card, reading, and turning pale*). What does she want, Charlotte? (*Charlotte shakes her head noncommittally*). Tell Mrs. Robinson that I will see her, Tabby. (*Tabby disappears right.*) Now, Charlotte, tell me what she wants. (*Both sisters are now upon their feet.*)

CHARLOTTE. The letter, perhaps. (*Pause.*) The shortest way to get rid of her, Anne, will be to give her what she wants, unless she wants —

ANNE (*comprehendingly, in a low voice*). Branwell. It's only half past nine. He will not leave the Black Bull before eleven, Charlotte.

CHARLOTTE. If we wanted Branwell to be in by half past nine, we could count upon his not leaving the Black Bull before eleven. But —

ANNE. I know. We must get her out of the house at once. Even if Branwell shouldn't come, there is papa — and Emily.

CHARLOTTE. You are right. Papa and Emily must be here soon. (*As Anne turns toward the parlor*) Shall I come with you?

ANNE. No, thank you. I see clearest when I have no helps. (*She goes out right, closing the door.*)

CHARLOTTE (*To Tabby, who comes out from the parlor*). Mrs. Birch must be having a hard time, Tabby. Papa and Emily are very late.

TABBY. I knew Martha Birch would dawdle out of the world. It's like her.

CHARLOTTE. You should forget that now, Tabby.

TABBY. I'm not blaming her. It's the poor thing's last chance to keep other people waitin'.

CHARLOTTE. Don't pretend to be heartless, Tabby. Not to me.

TABBY. I'm not heartless. No, ma'am. I don't grudge her a place in heaven if the good Lord wants her there.

CHARLOTTE (*finding protest useless*). Tabby, take that lamp, and put it in the window of papa's study. It's a dark walk for him and Emily.

TABBY (*taking the lamp*). They can't lose their way, ma'am. Keeper's with 'em. That dog's as good as a lantern.

CHARLOTTE. All the same it's a very dreary walk beside the churchyard, and the lamp will show them that something alive is waiting for them beyond the graves.

TABBY. They shouldn't be afraid of tombstones by this time. There's Brontës enough under 'em. (*Exit, with lamp, into study. The parlor door is noiselessly opened, and Anne enters into the dim, candle-lit room, and approaches Charlotte, now standing by the mantelpiece.*)

ANNE. She wants the letter. I have told her that she shall have the letter if she will go at once.

CHARLOTTE. She doesn't want Branwell, then?

ANNE. What she really wants she doesn't know herself. She thinks she wants the letter.

CHARLOTTE (*firmly*). Let her go before she forms other wants. Lose no time, Anne. (*Anne goes out by the nearer door left. Charlotte, with bent head and hands clasped before her, paces the room several times with a leisurely but emphatic gait, stopping sometimes for a contemplative instant before the closed parlor door. At last, she goes to the corner window, rear, and peers out into the swathing darkness. In this position she fails to hear the creak of the garden door, as Branwell Brontë, in hat and dark cloak, enters wearily, yet quickly, and, crossing the room obliquely, throws himself into a large armchair adjacent to the parlor door. With a shapely hand, he plucks off his hat, and tosses the cloak back from a well-knit and supple figure. In the boscage of warm chestnut hair the features appear to be delicately molded. He looks at the moment younger, and yet far older, than his years; his face reveals a bitter lassitude in which despair and exasperation meet. Even in this inauspicious moment, however, the face is not unamiable nor unappealing. From the other side of the closed parlor door comes a distinct, recurrent little sound, the sound of a slender foot tapping nervously against the tiles of a fireplace. Branwell rises, opens the door, and looks in.)*

BRANWELL. Evelyn! *(No one who had seen the young man a moment before would have thought him capable of the clear, joyous resonance of this exclamation. He enters the parlor. An instant afterward the door is very definitely closed.*

Charlotte, apprised of Branwell's presence by the cry, turns suddenly, just in time to see the door close between her and his disappearing figure. She is deeply agitated. She moves forward to midstage, and meditates for several moments with both clasped hands pressed strongly against her bent forehead. Then she walks to the parlor door, and firmly grasps the knob with her right hand. But the firm right hand does not turn the knob. On the contrary, it loosens its hold, and Charlotte walks to the fireplace, where she stands motionless, a faint silhouette in the half light of the candles. Anne enters by the passage door, a letter in her hand. Her quick, exploring glance fails to detect Charlotte's presence, and, after an inappreciable pause, she goes to the parlor door, turns the knob noiselessly, and looks in. Charlotte's eyes are riveted upon Anne. Three seconds pass, then Anne, closing the door silently, turns a blanched face upon Charlotte, who crosses to meet her at center. They face each other on opposite sides of the work table.)

CHARLOTTE. You didn't go in — *either?*

ANNE (*with a suppressed cry*). *Either?* Then you knew, Charlotte?

CHARLOTTE. Yes.

ANNE (*indignantly*). You should have warned me, Charlotte.

CHARLOTTE. Yes, I should have warned you. But — I wanted to see if you would do what I did.

ANNE. Why?

CHARLOTTE. I wanted to feel a little less ashamed.

ANNE (*defending herself against the implication*). How could I go in? The letter was to keep her from Branwell, and Branwell was *there*. I will go in with you now.

CHARLOTTE. Sit down, Anne.

ANNE (*looking toward the parlor door*). We ought to stop that.

CHARLOTTE. Yes, we ought. Sit down. (*Anne glances at Charlotte; then the two seat themselves at opposite sides of the work table.*)

ANNE. Emily would not do this.

CHARLOTTE. No. I think that's why I'm doing it. Three minutes ago I had grasped that knob firmly, and I thought, "That grasp is Emily's," and I drew my hand away. Emily makes resolution terrible.

ANNE (*thoughtfully*). She makes irresolution terrible, Charlotte.

CHARLOTTE. Yes. Emily makes it hard to be either like her or unlike her. I felt that there was something in there that I couldn't — couldn't stop all at once. Anne, have you ever read on in a wicked novel when you knew you ought to stop?

ANNE. Charlotte!

CHARLOTTE. I am reading such a novel now, and I do not stop. Every second I say to myself: "At the end of the next minute, Charlotte Brontë, you will rise and go to that door and stop that conversation"; and at the end of that minute Charlotte Brontë is still in this chair.

ANNE. You have a strong conscience, Charlotte.

CHARLOTTE. My conscience is the drunken porter in *Macbeth*. He hears the knocking, always the louder knocking, and he takes another draught.

ANNE. The porter *did* rouse himself, Charlotte.

CHARLOTTE. Yes, so will my conscience. It will open the door when the knock is loud enough, when Emily knocks and papa.

ANNE. Do you believe that evil is really hatching there? (*She indicates the parlor.*)

CHARLOTTE. Really believe? What do I really believe? They should be safe in a minister's parlor. Besides, they have other protections. Either of them is weak enough to be taken perhaps. But is either of them strong enough to take? I believe nothing can come of it. I think that. I must think that. If I do not think that, I am a lost soul.

ANNE. Why don't you stop it, anyway?

CHARLOTTE (*very slowly, after a pause*). One doesn't get a chance every night to lie upon the rug outside the door.

ANNE (*in passionate self-defense*). I never felt like that — never.

CHARLOTTE. Are you sure, Anne? Quite sure?

ANNE. There are questions that are wrongs, Charlotte.

CHARLOTTE (*gently*). I take it back. I did not mean to wound you. (*Pause.*) Something is working out in there toward good or evil, something that I ought to stop or steer, and I am content — thirstily, lappingly content — to rest within its shadow.

ANNE (*shrinking*). Emily would not do that.

CHARLOTTE. For Emily there is no rift between the feeling and the judgment. The feeling would crouch. With me now it is the judgment that crouches.

ANNE (*almost inaudibly*). Mine, too; mine crouches,

too, Charlotte. (*The rear door opens, and Emily, without hat or wrap, comes in. She is followed by her dog, Keeper.*)

EMILY. Both here — in this dusk. I remember. You put the lamp in papa's study for us. I shall need it. (*She mounts the steps, enters the study, and returns with the lamp, which she places on the writing table. Emily, at first view, under lamplight, is less formidable than a listener to her sisters' conversation might have guessed. On the surface, she is merely a medium-sized, firm-featured body with a quiet voice.*)

CHARLOTTE. Papa went into his study?

EMILY. Yes. It has been a hard night for papa. Mrs. Birch died very unquietly.

CHARLOTTE. I shall not die that way.

EMILY. Nor I. One should not meet the great silence — noisily. (*She has taken some manuscripts from the drawer of the writing table, and prepares to read. The dog Keeper wanders restlessly about the room. He stops and snuffs at Branwell's door.*) Has Branwell come in?

CHARLOTTE AND ANNE (*after a pause, both together, a little nervously*). Yes.

EMILY (*watching the dog*). He is early. That is new.

Even Keeper hardly believes it. (*The dog, after brief uncertainty, stretches himself on the carpet outside Branwell's door. Charlotte, under inward stress, rises from her chair, and moves toward the fireplace.*)

CHARLOTTE. Do you want a fire, Emily?

EMILY. No. The room is quite warm enough for me. (*Pause.*) Branwell was quiet?

CHARLOTTE (*bending over to straighten the andirons*). Very quiet. (*A silence. The dog Keeper suddenly rises from his couch, goes to the parlor door, snuffs curiously, and, after an instant's suspense, lies down in front of it. The three sisters follow his movements attentively.*)

EMILY (*on her feet*). He never did that before.

CHARLOTTE (*quickly*). He is restless, Emily.

EMILY. When Keeper is restless, he goes outdoors. There is something unusual in that room. (*She moves toward the parlor door. Tension in Charlotte and Anne.*)

CHARLOTTE (*with a suppressed cry*). Emily!

EMILY (*turning quietly*). Well?

CHARLOTTE (*with an effort*). There is something you should know before you open that door.

EMILY. What should I know?

CHARLOTTE. Branwell is there. He is busy with—another person.

EMILY (*curtly*). Who?

CHARLOTTE. Mrs. Robinson.

EMILY (*stepping back in amaze*). Mrs. Robinson! You have equivocated with me, Charlotte.

CHARLOTTE. That is a hard word, Emily.

EMILY. I use true words, hard or soft. You should have told papa of this woman's presence the instant he came in.

CHARLOTTE. Papa has been in only two minutes.

EMILY. Two minutes can do no end of mischief.

CHARLOTTE. What shall you do?

EMILY. What you would have done already if you had had a shred of character. I shall tell papa. Unless, indeed, I can make Branwell tell him. Get up, Keeper. (*Even in her present concentration she lays her hand affectionately upon Keeper's muzzle, and the dog licks her hand. Emily opens the door. Anne rises.*)

ANNE. Mrs. Robinson asked for me first, Emily. She wanted this letter.

EMILY. That can wait, Anne. (*She knocks at the parlor door. After several seconds it is opened by Branwell, who, seeing Emily, steps out and closes*

*the door carefully behind him. The brother and
sister face each other.*)

BRANWELL. What do you want with me, Emily?
(*The tone is low, mellow, gently satirical, but imperfectly assured.*)

EMILY. Just an answer to this question, Branwell: Is
it to be I or you who shall tell papa the name of
your present visitor?

BRANWELL (*temporizing*). Must papa know the
names of all my visitors?

EMILY. I am not thinking of all your visitors, Branwell. I am thinking of Mrs. Robinson.

BRANWELL (*pleadingly*). Give us half an hour. Give
us a quarter of an hour. She shall go then. I prom-
ise it.

EMILY. Papa shall give you as many quarter hours
as he pleases.

BRANWELL. Papa has no intelligence on some points.

EMILY. However dull your father may be, the house
is his house.

BRANWELL. Say a word for me, Charlotte.

EMILY. Yes, let us hear Charlotte's mind upon that
subject. (*She looks firmly, almost sternly, at her
sister.*)

CHARLOTTE. Emily — (*The word might be the pre-*

lude to an appeal for indulgence to Branwell, but the appeal does not follow. Charlotte, less in obedience to Emily's will than in a sudden revival of the activity of her own conscience, turns resolutely to Branwell.) Branwell, Emily is perfectly right. Whatever arrangements you may make with this woman, it is impossible for you to make them in papa's house without papa's knowledge.

BRANWELL (*quietly*). One never does the impossible, Charlotte.

CHARLOTTE. Never in this house.

BRANWELL (*appealingly*). Anne! (*Anne shakes her head. Branwell surveys the three musingly, as they stand in an approach to a semicircle in front of him, then meditates aloud.*) The ring of steel — the ring of steel — the ring of steel! (*It is characteristic of Branwell's temper that of the three exclamations the least emphatic and the dreamiest should be the third.*) Very well. Papa shall know. (*He moves with his alertest, proudest step toward the study, mounts the steps, and knocks. After a short interval the door is opened, and Patrick Brontë, white-haired, bearded, and rudely majestic, faces his four children.*)

BRANWELL. Emily has a message for you, father. (*He precedes his father down the steps.*)

MR. BRONTË (*whose gait, like his person, is imposing*). What have you to say to me, Emily? (*For an instant Emily, hastily gathering her thoughts, does not reply. Mr. Brontë's tone sharpens.*) Will you answer my question, Emily?

EMILY (*indicating the parlor door*). The answer is in there, papa.

MR. BRONTË. In there? How in there? I do not love mysteries. (*He scans the group frowningly, but crosses the stage, opens the parlor door, and closes it firmly behind him. Branwell looks long and steadily at the unmoving door, then turns away.*)

BRANWELL. You have succeeded, Emily. (*The tone, though anything but cheerful, is almost good-humored.*)

EMILY (*moving toward the desk*). I wasn't seeking success, Branwell.

BRANWELL. You were all the luckier, then. (*He crosses to fireplace, and looks into its unlit hollow. Emily seats herself at the writing table; Charlotte and Anne sit not far apart near the work table. Pause.*)

CHARLOTTE (*with a certain force*). You should master these passions, Branwell.

BRANWELL. You might just as well tell me to put out the fire in this grate. I have no passions, Charlotte. That is what happens when one grows up between the tombstones and the moors.

CHARLOTTE. We have all grown up there.

BRANWELL. I know. It has happened to all of us.

CHARLOTTE. Has it?

BRANWELL. I used to dream as a boy that the tombstones wanted to come into the house. They have come into the house. I have seen them — under the lids of women's eyes.

EMILY (*who has resumed her work with the manuscripts, but now pauses.*) We have done you no hurt whatever, Branwell. There is no happiness behind that closed door for you.

BRANWELL. There, you are quite right. When the door opens, it will let in something very different from happiness for me.

ANNE. What will it let in?

BRANWELL. Papa and your visitor, Anne. Papa will not spare her a last glance at the man who let his father and three sisters step between him and what he called his love for her. He will not spare me that — papa is very shrewd. After that she will be glad not to see me again, and I shall be glad not to be seen. We shall all be content — even papa, even Emily — even the tombstones.

EMILY (*with force*). Branwell, at bottom you are glad to have us step between you and that woman. If you are honest, you should thank us.

BRANWELL (*with a faint smile*). You see I am not even honest, Emily. (*With more energy.*) But perhaps you are right. Have I ever wanted anything intensely — intensely and long?

CHARLOTTE (*low-voiced*). I have.

BRANWELL (*ruminatively*). At the brim of the cup I have dreamt that there was joy in woman. In the arms of woman I have sometimes told myself that there was ecstasy in the cup. But the thing against my lip, the thing within my arms, has never held me.

EMILY. Why do you seek them, then?

BRANWELL. Why? One must imagine a good in something. But that isn't all. Should I tell you of things that I hardly grasp myself? You are women, you are sensitive, you write, and yet you could not understand it. It is a strange thing. There is something not me — not me, you understand me — that finds release through me.

CHARLOTTE. Something? What thing? (*Her voice is tense.*)

BRANWELL. How should I know? There is no answer to that question. When I go to the Black Bull, other feet than mine tread the path before me — yes, and they outrun mine. At the table other lips than mine approach the cup — taste it more eagerly than I. Other hands than mine clasp the dicebox — *with my fingers;* and eyes that are neither mine nor my companions' watch hungrily the resulting score. (*Charlotte and Anne listen eagerly; Emily bites her lower lip.*)

ANNE (*leaning forward breathlessly*). Whose eyes, whose hands, Branwell?

BRANWELL. I do not know. I am the flue by which passions that are not mine reach the surface, find their escape, blackening the track by which they go. They sustain and urge, and all at once they let me fall. Even here — tonight — as I sat in that room with Evelyn, I felt, not in myself, not even in that room, but around me — in the house, as it were — what shall I call them? — stringencies, urgencies, buoying me up and pressing me on. *They* made love to her, I — poor fool — fancying that it was I. When I came out, it all fell away; there was only the ring of steel — and papa's door knob. And of what I called passion there is now left only strength enough to hope that papa will not let that woman see what he and you — the three of you — have made of me. Emily was right about the gladness. (*With his old sad insouciance.*) Emily is a very intelligent woman.

EMILY (*rising, coming to Branwell, and laying her hand, not without grave kindness, upon his shoulder*). Trust my intelligence for one thing, Branwell. If these things are visitations, they can be mastered. Even one's own passions can be quelled.

BRANWELL. That is what the passionless say.

EMILY. Meaning me, and Anne, and Charlotte?

BRANWELL. I have no other sisters.

EMILY (*returning to her place at the writing table*). Perhaps you do not even know the sisters that you have.

BRANWELL. You live between the tombstones and the moors.

CHARLOTTE. What does that prove? The moors have their time to be purple.

ANNE. They *reek* with purple—in the summer.

CHARLOTTE. Even in the fall and winter the purple sleeps somewhere in their fibers, in their roots.

BRANWELL. With you it is all in your writings. There are pages in your books between which, if one pressed a snowdrop, he would take it out months later veined with scarlet. But I—but I—there is not fire enough in me to warm even a page.

CHARLOTTE. If you are as cold as you say, why all these dissipations? To drink without thirst, what can be more illogical?

BRANWELL. Sometimes one thirsts for thirst, Charlotte. One seeks the thirst in the bowl. But one doesn't find it.

CHARLOTTE. Is that why you go to the Black Bull?

BRANWELL. Mostly. I go to the Black Bull to imagine how pleasant it might be there—for a fellow that liked it.

EMILY. Is that why you courted Mrs. Robinson?

BRANWELL. You don't understand, yet you are the explanation—very largely. I am a gasp for air. That is not so wrong in an airless household. But I am a futile gasp. That is why papa is quite right in taking away my visitor.

CHARLOTTE. Anne's visitor.

BRANWELL. Quite right. I had forgotten. For Mrs. Robinson I am merely an interval between Anne and papa. Intervals are tedious things.

ANNE (*willing to change the subject*). Papa stays a long time.

EMILY. Are you impatient, Anne?

ANNE (*simply*). I am anxious that she should go.

CHARLOTTE. Papa is very quick with people whom he doesn't like.

BRANWELL. He is not quick with her. The conclusion is evident. Since we are to wait indefinitely — (*He moves upstage, sits down on the topmost of the three steps, takes a small volume from his pocket, and begins to read.*)

CHARLOTTE. You can see nothing at that distance from the lamp, Branwell.

BRANWELL. This is a book I can read with my fingers.

EMILY. Charlotte, come here a minute. Are these *your* verses? (*Charlotte goes to Emily, and looks at the manuscripts. The parlor door opens, and Mr. Brontë appears. He pauses on the threshold, as his eye meets Anne's. Then he looks back into the parlor.*)

MR. BRONTË. Will you come out into the living room, Mrs. Robinson? My daughter Anne is here. (*The lady who now enters the room is tall and hand-some, and is plainly many years older than the younger Patrick Brontë. While her face is not unamiable, it suggests neither emotional nor intellectual force; nevertheless, she has precisely the dignity and self-command which qualify her for her part in the ceremony which the elder Brontë is arranging. Branwell's head is averted; his eye does not forsake the printed page. Anne has risen.*)

MR. BRONTË. Anne, have you the letter which you showed me this morning?

ANNE. Yes, papa. (*She hands Mr. Brontë the letter.*)

MR. BRONTË. Mrs. Robinson, at my daughter's request I have read this note. You will agree with me that it is capable of two interpretations. Placed in Mr. Robinson's hands by you, it is capable of only one — the one in which I and my entire family concur. Mr. Robinson cannot but appreciate the speed with which you put yourself upon the track of the missing document, and the promptness with which you came back when an

old man showed his faith in you by restoring it.
(*He offers the note with his courtliest bow.*)

EVELYN ROBINSON. You are kind beyond my hopes —
beyond my deservings, Mr. Brontë. (*Her voice is
low and gracious.*)

MR. BRONTË. Mr. Robinson, I hope, will not be displeased to hear that you were met and welcomed
by my other daughters. Charlotte! Emily! (*The
two elder daughters come forward, both looking
intently into the guest's face.*) Charlotte, you will
give your hand to Mrs. Robinson. (*Charlotte,
after a moment's recoil, holds out her hand with
a look akin to eagerness.*) Emily! (*Emily, in
marked contrast with Charlotte, holds out her
hand with a gesture that is as decided as it is cold.*)

EVELYN ROBINSON. I am very glad to meet you. I have
heard so much of both of you from your sister
and — from Miss Anne, I would say.

MR. BRONTË (*turning his glance upon his son*). There
is still another member of my family who will
blame me if he is not allowed to greet you. Branwell! (*Under the cloak of conventional politeness
the voice bristles with command and menace, as
if the father saw and forestalled the son's impend-
ing mutiny. Branwell Brontë, keeping the book*

*in his hand, rises alertly to his feet. There is a
sudden light in his eye as of a man capable of
drawing a woman to his side with a vehemence
which should sweep filial piety and social scruple
into the dust heap. But his eye turns, as if in
appeal, to the three sisters, and his impulse shatters itself against what he perceives, or fancies, to
be the rock of their unbending disapproval. His
mood changes. Without lifting his eyes to Mrs.
Robinson's face, he bows low with a studied
courtesy and gentleness like a man who, with a
touching and resigned humility, bids a last and
hard goodbye to self-respect. Charlotte's hand
meets Anne's in an impassioned clasp; Emily remains impassive.)*

EVELYN ROBINSON *(who has courtesied in response
to Branwell's greeting).* Mr. Robinson and I have
both found much to esteem in Mr. Branwell
Brontë. *(Her eyes linger briefly on the young
man's face.)*

MR. BRONTË. I will tell your coachman to drive round
to the front entrance. *(He goes out by the parlor
door. Branwell Brontë and Mrs. Robinson still
face each other. Charlotte and Anne instinctively
retire down stage, but Emily keeps her place and*

does not divert her steady eyes from the man and woman.)

EVELYN ROBINSON. Goodbye, Mr. Brontë.

BRANWELL. Go back to Robinson, Evelyn. He is, at least, a man.

EVELYN ROBINSON. I shall always remember you.

BRANWELL. Forgetfulness would be kinder. What must you think of me?

EVELYN ROBINSON. Nothing that it would be hard for you to know. (*She turns from him, as Mr. Brontë re-enters.*)

MR. BRONTË. The carriage is waiting, Madam. May I have the honor? (*He offers his arm.*)

EVELYN ROBINSON. Thank you. (*She salutes the three sisters, who respond with varying shades of cordiality; then she leaves the room with Mr. Brontë.*)

BRANWELL (*to the three sisters*). Well, you have had your way — you and papa.

CHARLOTTE (*now standing by the work table*). What else could papa have done, Branwell?

BRANWELL. Nothing. His way and your way is, at bottom, my way, too. It is Evelyn's way. We are both glad that this has happened.

ANNE. Then why —

BRANWELL. Of course there is the shame of being

glad for such a reason — glad for being whipped into virtue. That shame will stay with one, dine and sup and wake and sleep with one forever. I shall get an hour or two of sleep tonight, and in that sleep I shall despise myself for sleeping. My dreams will be desolate. Goodnight.

ANNE (*impulsively*). Shall you dream of her, Branwell?

BRANWELL. No, not of her. I shall dream of the Erinyes. Sisters, you remember, and three of them. Goodnight. (*With a gesture that is half melancholy, half debonair, he enters his room, closing the door behind him. Emily sits down resolutely and resumes her work.*)

ANNE. If he knew, Charlotte!

CHARLOTTE (*looking after Branwell*). Yes, if he knew.

EMILY. What should he know?

CHARLOTTE. If I told you, Emily, could you understand — and forgive?

EMILY. Understand? Yes. About forgiving I am not so certain.

CHARLOTTE. I agree with you in every point about this matter. He and that woman could not have been happy together for a day — even putting the wickedness aside.

EMILY (*coldly*). I am glad you see that.

CHARLOTTE. I do see it. I would have given my right hand, I honestly think, to save him from this desperate mistake. At the same time—

ANNE (*coming to Charlotte, and throwing an arm around her waist*). Do not tell her, Charlotte.

CHARLOTTE. You felt that way, too, Anne? (*Anne nods.*) Then I think I can tell Emily.

EMILY (*elbow on table, looking straight at her sisters*). What is all this about?

CHARLOTTE (*firmly*). I would have given my right hand to stop it; but I would also have given my right hand to have it happen. There is purple even in the moors, Emily. To see Branwell take that woman in his arms under papa's eyes and go off with her—that was what I wanted. (*She faces Emily, half in defiance, half in awe.*)

ANNE (*clinging to Charlotte, but looking into Emily's eyes*). That was what we both wanted, Emily.

EMILY (*in a low, dry, firm voice, as she gazes into space at the moment that she prepares to resume her manuscripts*). What do you suppose I wanted?

CURTAIN

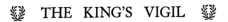

THE KING'S VIGIL

THE KING'S VIGIL

━━━━━━━━━━━━━━━━━━━━━━━━━━━

CHARACTERS

CHARLES THE SECOND, *King of England*

CATHARINE OF BRAGANZA, *Queen of England*

BARBARA PALMER, LADY CASTLEMAINE, *afterwards Duchess of Cleveland, the King's mistress and lady in waiting to the Queen*

THE EARL OF SANDWICH, *director of the fleet*

SAMUEL PEPYS, *clerk in the Navy Office*

ELIZABETH PEPYS, *his wife*

SUSAN, *their servant*

ANNE, *waiting maid at the Dutch Embassy*

The place is London; the period, springtime, 1662, two years before the actual outbreak of the Dutch War in 1664. The action occupies eleven hours. Scene One is at seven P. M., Scene Two at eleven P. M.; Scene Three at four of the next morning.

SCENE I

The dining room in Samuel Pepys's house at seven o'clock in the evening. Square room with exits to hall at back center, to parlor at left, and to kitchen at right. Furniture a little worn, but tasteful and dignified. A spinet in upper left-hand corner. Small sofa down stage right. Above the hall door, mantel with clock. Above the clock, copy of a Holbein. Other prints on the walls. Susan enters from the kitchen to Mrs. Pepys, as the curtain rises. Mrs. Pepys, slender, handsome, and still young, with a crispness extending from her toilet and her profile to her voice, sits on chair at left of table. She is very pointedly idle.

SUSAN. Master has come, ma'am.

MRS. PEPYS (*very calm, and, as it were, piously grateful for the unexpected*). He has come? Put on the dinner, Susan.

SUSAN. Yes, ma'am. (*She goes out right. Pepys, in business suit, but otherwise punctiliously groomed, enters from rear center. He is full of imperfectly repressed self-satisfaction.*)

MRS. PEPYS (*rising with an elaborate courtesy*). Mr. Pepys, I think.

PEPYS (*ignoring this demonstration, and taking his wife in his arms*). I am here, wife, God be thanked.

MRS. PEPYS (*submitting to the caress, but freeing herself quickly*). If you are here, it is God and not you that I have to thank for it. (*She looks at the clock; Pepys's eye follows hers.*)

PEPYS. It's only seven o'clock.

MRS. PEPYS. It might so easily have been eight. That is true. But the dinner is spoilt.

PEPYS. No matter for that. I had meat at Whitehall.

MRS. PEPYS (*dazzled out of her part for a moment*). Sam!! (*Recovering herself.*) Oh, yes, at White-hall. (*Meek and round-eyed.*) That is where the King lives, isn't it?

PEPYS. Where should the King live but in his own palace?

MRS. PEPYS (*raising deprecatory hands*). What should a poor housewife know about palaces, Mr. Pepys? When we want to know, we ask our husbands. Where else they go we must not ask, but they are quick enough to tell us that they have been to Whitehall. Of course a man from Whitehall could not eat our foolish dinner. It is true that I made the pudding with my own hands.

PEPYS. I have news that is better than pudding.

MRS. PEPYS (*in a would-be masculine voice*). Yes, yes, what should a man — a *man* (*very gruff on* "*man*") do with pu-u-uddings? (*Resuming her ordinary voice.*) Yet let wives forget puddings, and husbands remember them fast enough.

PEPYS (*coming to her and attempting an embrace*).

My dear, I will eat your pudding — *now*. All the King's meat in my stomach shall not stop me.

MRS. PEPYS (*kissing him, and instantly removing both her lips and her person*). He will eat my pudding! He will eat my pudding — *now!* (*Great emphasis on the "now."*) With the King's meat in him! O, the sacrifices that a man makes for his wife!

PEPYS. Elizabeth Pepys is the best pudding-maker in London. I would eat one if it sent me to the grave. And I would come back here from the grave to eat another.

MRS. PEPYS. It would be simpler to put the pudding on the grave stone. (*Calling.*) Susan! (*Susan appears.*) Susan, Mr. Pepys will have nothing but the pudding. He has dined at Whitehall. (*She enunciates "Whitehall" with elaborate nonchalance.*)

SUSAN (*breathless*). At Whitehall? With the King? (*She gasps between awe and triumph.*)

MRS. PEPYS. I do not know. When you want to know about kings, Susan, you must ask Mr. Pepys. He is now a great man, but I presume he will tell you. (*Susan turns imploring eyes upon Pepys.*)

PEPYS. I dined at Whitehall, Susan, but not with the King, that is, not exactly.

SUSAN (*disappointed in the sensation she has been husbanding for cook*). Oh!

MRS. PEPYS. Never mind, Susan. I am sure Mr. Pepys will be more exact another time. Fetch the pudding. I don't want any dinner.

PEPYS (*with real anxiety*). But you must eat.

MRS. PEPYS. My dear, a woman whose husband dines at Whitehall has no need of food. She can live on the envy of her neighbors. (*Susan enters, serves pudding, and goes out. Pepys seats himself at right of table, and begins to eat pudding. Mrs. Pepys takes seat at left of table.*) Now you must tell me everything.

PEPYS. Aha! We *do* want to know things after all.

MRS. PEPYS. Of course when people want to tell things, one has to ask them.

PEPYS. Wife, I was in secret consultation with the King this afternoon — for three hours.

MRS. PEPYS. Alone?

PEPYS (*chafed*). No, no, how should I be alone with the King? I am naught but a clerk.

MRS. PEPYS. Indeed! I thought the King would be making you Lord Chancellor.

PEPYS. Wife, wife, what frowardness is this! When good comes to a house, husband and wife should rejoice together.

MRS. PEPYS. They do, Pepys. Eat your pudding.

PEPYS (*resuming his spoon*). My Lord Sandwich was there and my Lord Albemarle and Sir George Carteret and some others — without titles.

MRS. PEPYS (*demurely*). One forgets those people.

PEPYS. We were Navy men, all of us, and the King besought our advice about the Dutch War.

MRS. PEPYS. Are we going to fight the Dutch, then?

PEPYS (*with a certain embarrassment*). My Lord Sandwich and my Lord Albemarle will have it so.

MRS. PEPYS. And the King?

PEPYS (*uneasily*). The King has no mind to war. He said he had no will to take English lads out of furrows and tumble them into graves.

MRS. PEPYS. English mothers will pray for a king like that.

PEPYS (*still uneasily*). Ay, ay, but my Lord Sandwich and my Lord Albemarle will have it that we go to war. They bade me show the King that the Navy was in trim to fight. Woman, I stood up there among the lords before the King, and talked, and the King heard me for all the world as if Sam

Pepys had been a lord among the others. And that is not all.

MRS. PEPYS (*lifting her eyes, and lifting her hands a little in her lap*). Is there more?

PEPYS. The King called me by name three times — three times, Madam. He called me Mr. Pepys.

MRS. PEPYS. Mr. Pepys! Think of it! Now if I had been a king, I am sure I should have called you Mr. Needham or Mr. Tompkins or Mr. Barlow.

PEPYS. I shall eat no more of your pudding, Elizabeth. It was made by an irreverent and mocking woman. (*He pushes the pudding from him.*)

MRS. PEPYS (*joining Pepys, and stroking his shoulder, half caressingly, half banteringly*). Eat your pudding. (*Putting her hand on his forehead.*) Eat your pudding. Elizabeth is curst, but the pudding is a very affectionate pudding. (*Pleadingly.*) Elizabeth put all her kindness into the pudding, so that there is none left to sweeten her tongue. (*Pause.*) No? No? Ah, when a man has been called "Mr. Pepys" by the King, he will eat nobody's pudding. He will not listen to his wife; he will mind nobody but kings. (*She leaves Pepys, traverses the room with a woman's imitation of a stride, and says in a swashing voice*) Mr. Pepys! Mr. Pepys! Mr. Pepys!

PEPYS (*furiously*). Elizabeth!

MRS. PEPYS (*same tone*). What, Mr. Pepys? (*Pepys pushes his chair back, as if to rise. Mrs. Pepys suddenly runs to her husband, seats herself on his knee, dips the spoon into the pudding dish, and feeds him mouthfuls between speeches.*) There, there, you shall be angry. You shall be very angry indeed, for I am a jealous little beast. If the King had called me "Mr. Pepys," I would never eat again unless my wife made the pudding. Did you tell the King what a nice wife you had?

PEPYS (*mollified*). That didn't come up.

MRS. PEPYS. No, no, these Dutch wars are very tedious. Did the King call you anything else but "Mr. Pepys?"

PEPYS. The last time it was "my good Mr. Pepys." Those were his words. I could swear to them.

MRS. PEPYS. Oh, if he said, "my good Mr. Pepys," after this there will simply be no living with you, (*she smooths a lock on his forehead*) no living with you. I shall run off with the greengrocer (he has pretty eyebrows). And when you come into the shop, I shall say to my new husband (that will be the greengrocer), "This is our good Mr. Pepys — our good Mr. Pepys — come to buy some cucumbers of us." I shall — I shall. (*She pecks at his forehead with her lips.*)

PEPYS (*putting his arm around her*). It is a great forward step for us, my dear. We must repaint the coach.

MRS. PEPYS. And brother Tom must have a new neckcloth. I have felt strongly for a long time about brother Tom's neckcloths.

PEPYS. We will send him a neckcloth and some silk stockings. The mercer has a new lot, some of which, being a little bleached in the heel, he will sell cheap. This is a high day for Samuel Pepys. Pray God it may be as good a day for England.

MRS. PEPYS. Why should the day be bad for England?

PEPYS. I think the King may go to war — against his own mind.

MRS. PEPYS. But if the Navy is ready? (*Pepys is silent and inscrutable.*) If the Navy is ready, Sam? (*Pepys continues silent and inscrutable.*) I thought you told the King that the Navy was in trim.

PEPYS (*slowly*). Kings are told many things.

MRS. PEPYS (*rising, but keeping a hand upon Pepys's shoulder*). What do honest men tell them?

PEPYS. Honest men say what their betters bid them say. If they didn't, soon there would be no honest men in England — but the beggars.

MRS. PEPYS. Then the Navy isn't ready? (*She removes her hand. Pepys shrugs his shoulders.*) Why do these lords want to go to war if their Navy isn't ready? (*She returns to her own side of the table, and faces Pepys.*)

PEPYS. The war will go wrong for a time, and that will turn out my Lord Chancellor.

MRS. PEPYS. He should be a good man who has to be turned out by a war and a lie.

PEPYS. You say true, wife. I was ill pleased to tell the King less than the whole truth — on a day, too, when he had been so kind to me. But what would you have? God himself would have been a sinner in my case.

MRS. PEPYS. So, you have made God a sinner! You will make the devil a saint next.

PEPYS. The two come close enough in a man's wife.

MRS. PEPYS. I made my pudding for an honest Englishman.

PEPYS. And what would your honest Englishman

eat, after he had lost his place? Acorns? There is no Englishman honest enough to like them.

MRS. PEPYS. I would eat acorns before I would tell the King that leaky ships were whole, and let him thank me. I would, Mr. Pepys. (*She utters the last words with a trace of the old sarcasm.*)

PEPYS. Listen to me. My heart is sad for England — sadder than a woman's; but it would be sadder still for Samuel Pepys if he were thrust out from his warm berth in the Navy, and he would think twenty times of Samuel for once that he now thinks of England. There is no reason in women — though the creatures are pleasant enough, when they are pleased to be silent.

MRS. PEPYS. No, there is no reason in women; otherwise, they would agree with men. (*Susan appears at door back.*)

SUSAN. My Lord Sandwich, Mr. Pepys.

PEPYS (*starting up*). Impossible!

SUSAN. He *says* he's my Lord Sandwich.

MRS. PEPYS. Clear the table, Susan. Mr. Pepys will fetch in my Lord Sandwich himself. (*She straightens the furniture.*)

PEPYS (*embarrassed*). He has come on business, wife.

MRS. PEPYS (*not without suspicion*). You expected him?

PEPYS. No, but he has much to do, and men like him have no time for men like me on busy days except for business.

MRS. PEPYS (*looking at her gown*). This is the frock I put on to make the pudding. You think he would notice?

PEPYS (*anxious to have her go, but also to hide this anxiety*). You look very well. But my Lord Sandwich *is* critical of women's frocks. You see, Lady Sandwich never makes puddings.

MRS. PEPYS. I had best go. (*She goes out left; Pepys goes out back, and returns in a moment, ushering the Earl of Sandwich, a plump, florid, middle-aged Englishman, with a mien of high self-confidence and hearty ease.*)

PEPYS. Your lordship condescends to an unworthy servant.

SANDWICH. Not at all. I've often thought of coming to see you, Pepys, but, like most men, I never do the things I want to till I have to. That's a Holbein, I'll swear. (*Points to the space above rear door.*) By my life, you commoners snap up everything nowadays while we peers are putting on our eyeglasses. Pepys, I want to sit down, and I hope that sofa in the corner is only half as comfortable as it looks. (*Pepys deferentially conducts Sandwich to the sofa, and, after an obsequious interval, sits down in a chair to the left of Sandwich.*)

PEPYS. May I offer your lordship a glass of wine? Madeira? 1650?

SANDWICH. No, thanks. For once I am proof even against Madeira. Everything went finely this afternoon.

PEPYS. I am thankful to have pleased your lordship.

SANDWICH. The King was pleased — that's more to the purpose. The King likes you. After you left us, he praised your handwriting.

PEPYS (*in a deeply gratified tone*). His Majesty is too good.

SANDWICH (*incidentally*). He called attention to your H's.

PEPYS (*with a deep, indrawn breath*). Ah! (*Then, anxiously.*) He said nothing about my Y's?

SANDWICH. On the Y's I do not remember that his Majesty was particular. He has had a very busy day.

PEPYS. Certainly, certainly, the Y's can wait. It is not

that I value my own Y's, Lord Sandwich, but they
have been well spoken of by thoughtful judges.

SANDWICH. The King remembered your name.
"Pepys — a good, short name," he said. "Short as
a king's memory," replied my Lord of Buckingham. "A king has no need of memory, George,"
replied his Majesty; "he has so many reminders."
Then we all laughed, because Buckingham had
been pressing upon the King a cornetship in the
Guards that he wanted for a second cousin.

PEPYS (*with instant curiosity*). Did he get the cornetship?

SANDWICH. Why, yes. The King had refused, but
was so pleased with the success of his *bon mot*
that he changed his mind and gave it after all.
Buckingham had laughed the loudest.

PEPYS (*with a shade of disapproval*). A cornetship
is high pay for a laugh.

SANDWICH (*ignoring the disapproval*). I must tell
you of another good thing they were telling in the
corridors today. You know the King's spaniels?

PEPYS. I have seen them in the park.

SANDWICH. Bennet, the pleasant fellow that has just
come up, said to Lord Ashley the other day:
"There is nothing the King won't do for his

spaniels. I wonder he doesn't make councillors of them." Ashley looked at him sidewise, and said: "I thought he did." (*Sandwich laughs; Pepys follows with a respectfully distant heartiness, an "After you, Sir" brand of laugh.*)

PEPYS. The Court was never so gay as now, sir.

SANDWICH. The war will sober us. We are practically sure of the war. Your figures impressed the King.

PEPYS. I wished I had been more sure that the King understood my figures.

SANDWICH. Never mind as to that. It is not the King's business to understand figures. The King's business is to look at columns of accounts, nod out of weariness, and allow his councillors to read affirmatives into the nod.

PEPYS. There is small comfort in that for England.

SANDWICH. England! Nonsense, my dear Pepys! We will comfort England some other time. Look here. I know and Albemarle knows that there's plenty of rottenness in the Navy from the bulkheads up to the budgets, but what of that? England can't *lose* a war, and if she gets a few hard knocks in the beginning, it will serve her right and do her good.

PEPYS. Your lordship is always right.

SANDWICH (*with good-humored bluffness*). Where am I wrong now, Pepys?

PEPYS (*with great deference*). You are wrong in thinking that I could differ from your lordship. If I were talking to a man no wiser than myself — (*he pauses to look at Sandwich, who nods toward him with a half quizzical encouragement*) I should have reminded him (*again the look and the responsive nod*) — that our ships are but half manned, and manned often, at that, with fellows that are but half seamen, that we run low in powder, and that half our keels are so patched and plugged that they have more reason to fear the North Sea than the Dutch cannon.

SANDWICH (*coolly*). We are not prepared. We all know that.

PEPYS (*looking Sandwich in the face with a certain courage*). Except the King.

SANDWICH. The King mustn't know it. And the want of preparation will do no real harm.

PEPYS (*with a studiously incidental air*). It might take lives.

SANDWICH. War takes lives as a matter of course.

England is unprepared. She always was. Never prepared, but always ready — that is England.

PEPYS. I could wish she were always prepared and never ready.

SANDWICH. That may do for the twentieth century. At that time, we may presume, Lord Clarendon will not be Lord Chancellor of England. Our present business is to get rid of him.

PEPYS. It takes a war to do it?

SANDWICH. Just that.

PEPYS. He must be a faithful servant of the Crown if it takes a war to put him out.

SANDWICH. A faithful servant? Of course he is. But he is very much in the way of some other faithful servants of the Crown of whom I chance to be one. We must have the Dutch war. The King was half won by your figures this afternoon; Lady Castlemaine will do the rest tonight.

PEPYS (*half rising from his chair, then abruptly re-seating himself*). Lady Castlemaine!

SANDWICH. Lady Castlemaine will meet the King tonight. She will persuade him to fight the Dutch.

PEPYS (*with great interest*). Lady Castlemaine hates the Dutch, then, my lord?

SANDWICH. Not at all. She hates the Chancellor.

PEPYS (*cautiously*). I thought the King had left off seeing Lady Castlemaine.

SANDWICH. Quite right. The King has had to be cautious. Portugal is friendly to the Dutch — both deadly enemies of Spain. Portugal must not take their side in a Dutch war. The Queen's messages to Portugal at this moment must not inflame that country against England.

PEPYS (*who has been drinking all this in*). The King, then, must spare the Queen's feelings —

SANDWICH (*with courtierlike cynicism*). When they happen to be also the feelings of Portugal.

PEPYS. How, then, can he go to Lady Castlemaine tonight?

SANDWICH. He will not go to her lodgings. There is always a crowd in the street. He will meet her in Whitehall — secretly. You remember those suites for foreign visitors, parlor with sleeping room attached?

PEPYS. Yes, my lord. I have been making use of one of them for office work in this Navy matter. I have no further use for the key. Shall I hand it to your lordship?

SANDWICH. Keep it till you've removed the papers. As I was saying, Lady Castlemaine and the King will meet tonight, by our contrivance, in one of these neglected suites. Everything will be secure by morning.

PEPYS (*suddenly rising and speaking with impulsive vehemence*). My lord, this is no act for — (*He stops suddenly.*) I beg your pardon, my lord — I was about to say something which your lordship could not have forgiven.

SANDWICH (*watching with a feline good nature the struggle between indignation and servility in Pepys*). Say it, and I forgive you.

PEPYS (*imploringly*). My lord!

SANDWICH. Don't say it, and I don't.

PEPYS. My first thought was that it was no act for honest men.

SANDWICH. Sit down, Pepys. (*Pepys sits down.*) We had to bring them together. I grant the thing has an ugly look. If I were a Navy clerk and could afford to be shocked, I should be shocked myself. Lady Castlemaine was the only way. Remember that it's the King's habits, not ours, that make her the only way. Have you been on board ship, Pepys?

PEPYS. Three times, my lord.

SANDWICH. That is better than some of our admirals.

In that case you have seen a deck swept, and swept clean, by a dirty broom.

PEPYS. Very true, but it always left the sweeper dirty.

SANDWICH (*laughing*). Very good. I am sorry I can't tell that to the King. Lady Castlemaine is the jest of the kingdom, and she is the only subject on which the merriest Englishman alive declines to joke. But now to my business. You will receive a messenger from the Dutch Embassy tonight.

PEPYS. What kind of messenger?

SANDWICH. That I don't know, but I can tell you what he will bring. Someone has been furnishing the Dutch ambassador with information about the state of our Navy.

PEPYS. Do you know who?

SANDWICH. No. But a message from this unknown source will reach the Embassy tonight. The ambassador will not read the message till tomorrow morning. We have an agent in the Embassy who will give us the loan — the loan, mind you — of the manuscript for a few hours tonight. It must be read — and copied — and returned.

PEPYS. I am to do that?

SANDWICH. Yes. You see, it's probably in shorthand.

You must find some way of returning the original to the Embassy before midnight.

PEPYS. Would it not be best to keep it?

SANDWICH. The paper will not be signed. The correspondence must go on so that we may discover the writer. (*Pepys nods with quick intelligence.*) And you must not return the paper to the Embassy yourself. You see, don't you? — that would put them on our track. (*Pepys nods briskly.*)

PEPYS. But it is ill for us that the Dutch should know the weakness of our Navy.

SANDWICH. Certainly. But we have this consolation, Pepys. It is more important that the King shouldn't know than that the Dutch should, and the Dutch can be trusted for one thing — not to pass on the information to the King.

PEPYS. I shall do your lordship's pleasure.

SANDWICH. And now, having discharged my commission, I must be gone. Will you assure Mrs. Pepys of Lady Sandwich's high regard? (*He goes to door back.*)

PEPYS (*following Sandwich*). She will be most humbly grateful. Goodnight, my lord. (*Sandwich goes out. Pepys returns to table, and stands tap-*

ping the table with his left hand as he reflects. Susan enters at door right.) Well, Susan?

SUSAN. There is a person in the kitchen, sir. (*Susan's pronunciation of the word "person" puts it in quarantine, so to speak.*)

PEPYS. Person? (*He reflects again.*) Not from the Dutch Embassy?

SUSAN. Yes, sir. A woman.

PEPYS (*astonished*). A woman? Why didn't you take her in to Mrs. Pepys?

SUSAN (*very promptly*). She wasn't Mrs. Pepys's kind of woman.

PEPYS (*a light breaking on him*). Young? (*Susan nods. Pepys sighs.*)

SUSAN. Worse than that, sir.

PEPYS. Not pretty? (*Susan nods emphatically. Pepys sighs more deeply.*) Susan, why are so many women young and pretty?

SUSAN. God knows — or the devil. Shall I fetch her in?

PEPYS (*resignedly*). Fetch her in. (*Susan, instead of moving right toward the kitchen, goes to the door left, which she closes with ostentatious precision, but without noise. Then she returns.*)

SUSAN (*in a comforting, housewifely voice, and giv-*

ing Pepys a look which defies him to accuse her of ulterior motives). I thought Mrs. Pepys might be asleep, sir.

PEPYS. Quite right. We won't disturb Mrs. Pepys.

SUSAN (*stopping at the table to lay hands upon the pudding dish*). I'll fetch the young person in, Mr. Pepys. (*Somehow there is a snub to the young person in the fashion in which Susan appropriates the pudding dish. She goes out right, leaving the door open. Pepys, looking toward the doorway, presently sees it filled by the figure of a young girl of humble station in an artlessly coquettish frock. Her bright eyes, red lips, and red cheeks make her undeniably pretty. She has a slyness of the most ingenuous sort and a timidity that waits only for a signal to put on confidence. Pepys takes in all these details in a single comprehensive and apprehensive glance, then fixes his eyes upon the Holbein with the air of a connoisseur besieged by a distracting world.*)

ANNE. Mr. Pepys?

PEPYS (*facing her again*). I am Mr. Pepys.

ANNE. For your own hand, sir. (*She hands him a large envelope. Pepys unseals it, extracts what appears to be several pages of a closely written short-*

*hand manuscript, scans it casually, yet keenly, and
replaces the sheets in the envelope. Then he turns
to Anne.*)

PEPYS (*in a carefully lowered voice*). I have to copy
this paper. You must come for it at eleven o'clock.

ANNE (*at right of table*). Here, sir?

PEPYS (*ruefully facing a new difficulty*). No. You
must come to my office in Whitehall. You know
Whitehall, girl? King Charles's palace?

ANNE (*dismayed by this prospect*). Why couldn't I
come here?

PEPYS (*approaching Anne*). Because I'm a married
man, and a married man mustn't have very young
and pretty visitors (*he rests his hand, as it were
casually, upon her hair*) — very young and very
pretty visitors, do you hear? (*he strokes her
hair*) — in his house at eleven o'clock.

ANNE (*blushing*). Ah, Mr. Pepys!

PEPYS (*pushing her away from him, but not un-
gently*). Don't Mr. Pepys me. I won't be Mr.
Pepysed. You must come to Whitehall — at eleven
o'clock.

ANNE. I couldn't come to Whitehall — alone. I
couldn't.

PEPYS. It's perfectly easy.

ANNE. I couldn't. (*Her voice has a hint of tears.*)

PEPYS. You shan't cry, do you hear? Mrs. Pepys allows no one to cry in her dining room. (*The pronunciation of this name has a fortifying effect upon Anne. She dries her eyes.*) Now look here. I'm going to give you the direction. (*Takes a card from his pocket, and writes, seated at table.*) Take boat from Embassy and get off at Whitehall stairs. (*He writes, and speaks as he writes.*) Second entrance at left — second, you understand? Right wing. Third corridor — third, mind you. Room 24. (*He hands the card to Anne, who surveys it with a profound air that Pepys finds suspicious.*) Well?

ANNE. I couldn't, Mr. Pepys. I couldn't really.

PEPYS (*solving the riddle*). You can't read? (*Anne nods.*) I might have guessed as much. Look here. I will draw a map for you. Sit down. (*Anne sits at the table beside him. Pepys takes more paper and sketches.*) You see here — the landing, and there is the door — and the stairs here — (*He stops suddenly, his eye wandering to the rosy cheek beside him; then he speaks severely.*) If you could contrive not to be so pretty —

ANNE (*hardly knowing what she says*). I'll do my best, Mr. Pepys, I really will.

PEPYS (*more kindly*). That's a good girl. Up the stairs, then — to the second story — down the main corridor — (*He interrupts himself.*) That is a very pretty neck you have.

ANNE (*with the air of one always open to new ideas*). Do you think so?

PEPYS (*with official dryness*). I am quite convinced of it. But we were talking business, my girl. Necks can wait.

ANNE (*taking this unjust reproof meekly*). Yes, Mr. Pepys.

PEPYS (*with dignity*). Down the main corridor — you get that?

ANNE. Ye-e-e-s.

PEPYS. Then turn into this passage — at the green archway — the green archway, mind — and so down to Room 24. You can tell it by the carved black door knob. (*Dreamily.*) It would look very pretty with a string of pearls around it — very pretty.

ANNE. The door knob, Mr. Pepys? (*Pepys, without replying, continues to look at her. Anne studies the diagram.*) I couldn't find it — I couldn't really.

PEPYS. Could you, if I offered you a string of pearls
   for coming?

ANNE (*in a moiling voice*). Pearls! I could do anything for pearls.

PEPYS. You will come? (*He puts his arm around
   her.*)

ANNE. Yes. (*But she suddenly stops in her contented
   surrender.*) But how should I get back?

PEPYS. Plenty of ways, plenty of ways. The barges
   run very late at night—(*pause*) and very early
   in the morning. (*Their eyes meet; then he kisses
   her on the lips.*)

ANNE (*in a whisper*). I must go.

PEPYS. Yes, go. (*He releases her, and they both rise.
   Anne, after a swift glance about the room which
   overlooks the diagram upon the table, runs to the
   entrance right, where pausing for a moment, she
   signals with a fond gesture to Pepys. Pepys waves
   an answering hand, as she goes out. When she
   has gone, he takes the envelope from his pocket,
   extracts the manuscript, and, sitting down at the
   table, rapidly fingers the sheets. Then he rises and
   goes toward the exit back. As he is about to pass
   out, Mrs. Pepys appears in the doorway left. Pepys
   turns, glances at her, goes out, and returns almost*

instantly with his hat and his light cloak in his hand. His wife is at left center, and he is now able to meet her eye with a show of coolness.)

MRS. PEPYS. You are going out, Pepys?

PEPYS. To Whitehall for my Lord Sandwich. He has a paper that I am to copy tonight. (*He points to the manuscript on the table; Mrs. Pepys goes to table, and inspects it.*)

MRS. PEPYS (*distrustful on principle, but a little dashed by the evident actuality of the manuscript*). Couldn't you copy it at home?

PEPYS. Yes, but the messenger is to call for it at Whitehall.

MRS. PEPYS. You will be back early?

PEPYS. Perhaps, but if Lord Sandwich has other work for me, I may spend the night at Whitehall.

MRS. PEPYS (*very genially*). It is well to be on hand. The King might miss you.

PEPYS (*placatingly*). He will not miss me so much as I shall miss my good wife.

MRS. PEPYS. One can see that Mr. Pepys has been to court. He is so very civil. You are forgetting your manuscript. (*Pepys had been putting on his cloak; Mrs. Pepys carries the manuscript to him.*)

PEPYS. Goodnight, my wife. A wife is a pleasant thing when she is friendly.

MRS. PEPYS (*in her sprightly way*). And a husband when he is truthful.

PEPYS (*affecting injury*). Am I not truthful, wife?

MRS. PEPYS. We shall see, husband, we shall see. (*He kisses her poutingly, as it were; she kisses him almost saucily. Then he goes out back. Mrs. Pepys, back to audience, stands in the doorway. From the kitchen, Anne enters in nervous haste. Her glance about the room is so cursory that it misses Mrs. Pepys, and in another instant her speed has brought her to the table, which she searches eagerly with eyes and fingers. Mrs. Pepys turns and sees her.*)

MRS. PEPYS (*kindly enough*). What is it?

ANNE (*greatly flurried*). The — the paper.

MRS. PEPYS. What paper?

ANNE. The paper — Mr. Pepys — gave me.

MRS. PEPYS (*approaching the table, and stooping to pick something from the floor*). Is this it? (*She retains the paper.*)

ANNE (*gaspingly*). Yes.

MRS. PEPYS (*examining the paper, and speaking very civilly*). What is it?

ANNE. Whitehall — his room.

MRS. PEPYS (*keenly, but still not unkindly*). You are to meet him there? When?

ANNE (*who is relieved, and yet discomfited, by Mrs. Pepys's extraordinary good nature*). At eleven o'clock tonight. (*Pause.*) I am to take the paper back to the Embassy.

MRS. PEPYS. The Dutch Embassy?

ANNE. Yes. I work there.

MRS. PEPYS. And you are going for this paper to Mr. Pepys's room in Whitehall at eleven o'clock tonight?

ANNE (*after some reflection*). Yes.

MRS. PEPYS (*still brisk and gracious*). That is all you are going for? Quite all?

ANNE (*too eager to fend off suspicion*). There are the pearls.

MRS. PEPYS. Pearls?

ANNE. He promised me a string of pearls.

MRS. PEPYS (*with great coolness, surveying Anne*). Pearls would look well on you.

ANNE (*delighted with this sympathetic lady*). That's what he said.

MRS. PEPYS. I have no doubt of it. My husband's judgment in these points is very good.

ANNE (*who is learning new things about wives every moment, in a contented undertone*). Yes.

MRS. PEPYS (*more and more genial*). But, my dear, you can't go to Whitehall alone tonight. I shall take you.

ANNE (*who has some excuse for thinking this proposition novel*). I think — I'd better go alone.

MRS. PEPYS (*robustly genial*). Nonsense! You can't find your way by this diagram.

ANNE (*who knows this is true, in a faltering voice*). I have to.

MRS. PEPYS (*putting the diagram before Anne*). Come now, tell me, which is the top and which is the bottom?

ANNE (*after a vain scrutiny*). I don't know.

MRS. PEPYS. You see. I shall take you myself in a coach.

ANNE (*to whom this proposal, in spite of its attractions, seems irregular and disturbing*). Thank you, but —

MRS. PEPYS (*putting her two hands on Anne's two shoulders*). Don't thank me. I want to make sure that you get your pearls. Mr. Pepys is very generous, but very absent-minded. I shall not allow him

to forget you. You are an excellent girl, and men
are very thoughtless.

ANNE (*tremulously*). But —

MRS. PEPYS. There! There! Think what a disappointment it would be not to have them to wear
to church with your best frock on Sunday morning.

ANNE (*yielding, like all of us, to the irresistible*).
It's very — very kind of you.

MRS. PEPYS. Don't say another word. I'll be at the
Embassy with a coach at half past ten. Good-
bye. (*She pilots Anne toward the entrance back.
At this moment Susan appears in the entrance
right.*) At half past ten. Goodbye, my dear.
(*Anne goes out. Mrs. Pepys turns and perceives
the amazed Susan.*) You needn't stay up, Susan.
There'll be nothing more for you to do tonight.

SUSAN (*still staring toward the exit through which
Anne has vanished*). Thank you, ma'am.

MRS. PEPYS (*observing Susan's fixity*). You noticed
that little woman who just went out, Susan? She's
a very nice little girl from the Dutch Embassy,
and Mr. Pepys and I are very fond of her.

SUSAN (*very respectfully*). Yes, ma'am.

CURTAIN

SCENE II

Whitehall at eleven o'clock the same evening.

The curtain rises slowly on a large room of rich, though faded, appointments — the main part of what was once known as a foreign visitor's suite. The suite consists of a spacious outer room which might serve alternately as boudoir or cabinet or parlor with a sleeping chamber in the rear which is approached by a deeply set, fairly massive, and rather noticeable door set exactly in the center of the high, frescoed, and wainscoted back wall. There are entrance doors at right and left. Desk in center of room with a broad, flat space for writing, ink, pens, and an adjoining easy chair. The back, left-hand corner of the stage is partly shut from view by a richly painted, many-sectioned, folding screen, so adjusted at the moment that fully half the corner, with a card table, two chairs, and other accessories, remains open to the eyes of the spectators. At the front left a large cabinet or cupboard set in the wall. On the right side in front of the entrance door, fireplace and mantelpiece with carvings and ornaments. Further back on the right deep, leather-covered, valanced sofa. Small table near sofa. Chairs at fit spots, large, low, and old. The frescoes noted on the back wall extend all around the room.

The curtain as it goes up reveals Pepys asleep in the easy chair beside the desk. His cloak and hat are on another chair a little farther upstage. On the desk are two tall lighted candles, and two manuscripts, the shorthand manuscript received from the Dutch Embassy resting neatly on the much bulkier longhand copy which Pepys has spent the evening in completing. A small, trim-looking paper box lies beside the manuscripts.

After a moment there is heard the sound of the insertion of a key from without in the door right. The seeker for entrance apparently discovers that the key is superfluous; he enters, turning to look with an evident misgiving at the unused key still clasped in his fingers and at the peccant door. The spectators find themselves looking sympathetically at a brown-faced, pleasant-looking man of thirty-two, who wears his royalty as unassumingly as his cape and bonnet. Charles the Second looks at the lighted candles with a surprise which for the moment prevents him from catching sight of Pepys. He walks with a quick stride to the bedroom door, where he is met by an exact reversal of his surprise a moment ago. The door will not yield to his unaided hand. The King has a key, which he takes from his pocket, cradles irreso-lutely in the palm of his right hand, and finally restores to the pocket. He then comes back to the center of the room, where his eye with a dismay which passes gradu-ally — and yet rapidly — into amusement, encounters the unconscious Pepys.

Lifting a candle from the table, he examines the sleeper's face with a curiosity to which half-recollection imparts new perplexities. He puts the candle down, and takes

*up the manuscripts. He makes nothing of the shorthand,
and is content to drop the longhand copy with a sigh
when he discovers that it relates to Navy business. These
attempts having whetted rather than dulled the instinct
of investigation, he takes up the little box, opens it, and
discovers a chain of small pearls which glimmer coyly in
the candlelight. The King lets it out into a string, then
gathers it into a coil with the skill of a hand that practice
has seasoned in the arts that win favors from women.
Then he turns with a divining smile to Pepys, delib-
erately lets out the string, and allows its extremity to
tease the end of Pepys's nose. Pepys stirs, sneezes a little,
and opens a pair of at first bewildered, and afterwards
terror-stricken, eyes upon his sovereign.*

THE KING (*with a delightful suavity*). You will excuse me for waking you?

PEPYS (*gasping*). Your — your — your Majesty! (*He
struggles to his feet in the effort to fall upon his
knees.*)

THE KING (*restraining him*). Do not kneel. The
rosettes on your hose are very smart, and the floor,
I think, is dusty.

PEPYS. If I had dreamed, your Majesty —

THE KING (*smiling*). Isn't that just what you were
doing? (*With real kindness.*) Do not distress
yourself. A peer or a valet in my situation might

have caned you, but I — I have learned meek-
ness — on a throne. My very spaniels bully me.

PEPYS (*pointing to the manuscripts*). I — I was
working for the Navy, sir.

THE KING. You could not spend your time more
loyally. Will you fetch me that chair? (*Pepys
fetches the chair to which the King points.*) And
now draw up your own. (*Pepys is deprecatory,
but the King quiets him by a gesture, and they
sit facing each other just in front of the desk.*)
I have seen you before. (*Pepys bows.*) This afternoon. (*Pepys bows again.*) At the Navy consultation. (*Pepys bows a third time.*) I remember
thinking you had an honest face. (*Pepys beams.*)
Your accounts were very lucid, Mr. — Mr. —
(*Pepys waits in delighted expectation.*) Mr. — I
seem not to recall the name.

PEPYS (*hardly audible from disappointment*). Pepys.

THE KING. Pepys! Yes. I don't know why I forgot.
It should not trouble a prince to remember the
names of all the honest men in his service. (*Pepys
is radiant again.*) And now, Mr. Pepys, how does
it happen that you and I are enjoying each other's
society — if I may assume — (*he glances roguishly
at Pepys*) that the enjoyment is mutual?

PEPYS. Lord Sandwich gave me a key. I was to prepare the accounts in this office.

THE KING (*musingly*). A key? There is a second key, then. But your work seems to be complete and you had fallen asleep. What were you waiting for?

PEPYS (*worried again*). I expected a messenger.

THE KING. Yes, yes, a messenger, why not? (*He looks fixedly at Pepys, then says casually.*) Does he like pearls? (*He holds up the string, which he has not relinquished.*)

PEPYS. The messenger?

THE KING. Yes.

PEPYS (*looking anxiously at the pearls*). I cannot say, your Majesty.

THE KING (*more gravely than heretofore*). Let me see your key. (*Pepys hands him a key.*) Have you a key to that door? (*He points toward the bedroom. Pepys, with a certain reluctance, produces a second key. The King, after inspecting it, hands back both keys to Pepys.*) Very well. You have convinced me that the messenger likes pearls.

PEPYS. I am a sinful man. I should not have shuffled with your Majesty.

THE KING'S VIGIL

THE KING (*in his most winning way*). I am the last person who could act as your censor, Mr. Pepys. Indeed I am proud to share my frailties with so good a subject. (*Pepys looks at him gratefully.*) One further question. You are married?

PEPYS. Yes. She is half French.

THE KING. I am half French myself. My mother was a Frenchwoman. She is pretty?

PEPYS. My Lord Sandwich does me the honor to say so.

THE KING. Sandwich should know. (*He meditates an instant.*) I wish the opinion of my peers were half so good on any practical subject as it is on profiles and complexions. (*Resuming the former topic.*) This messenger who likes pearls is not — I am bound to infer — Mrs. Pepys?

PEPYS. No. She likes jewels, however.

THE KING. That is probable.

PEPYS (*with a shade of pensiveness*). My wife is an excellent woman.

THE KING. So is mine. Excellence is the only quality which no woman begrudges to another. And the reason is plain.

PEPYS (*shyly*). What is the reason?

THE KING. It is the only quality that a man doesn't admire. Your wife suspects you?

PEPYS. Hardly, your Majesty. Up to now I have been true to her — almost.

THE KING (*smiling*). "Almost" is a tiny slit, but it is big enough to let the devil through.

PEPYS (*with a sigh*). Yes. (*The sigh amuses the King, but it rather touches him, too.*)

THE KING. You will pardon the curiosity of a — of a fellow-adventurer, Mr. Pepys. Who is the lady you expect tonight?

PEPYS (*mortified*). A — a housemaid.

THE KING. I had expected a countess. In England, you know, the countesses are very nearly as pretty as the housemaids.

PEPYS (*quite frankly*). One *sees* the housemaids.

THE KING. Quite true. Once more — I am very indiscreet, but you speak to a king whose subjects have pardoned him for a thousand indiscretions — you have met this young woman before?

PEPYS. I met her only today. There is really nothing between us. A kiss or two. You see, I had been fretted by my wife.

THE KING. I understand perfectly. You told me she

was an excellent woman. What particular virtue was uppermost today?

PEPYS. I had told her that this afternoon your Majesty spoke to me three time by name — three times.

THE KING (*smiling*). You are sure it wasn't four?

PEPYS (*firmly*). Three times. My memory of it is humbly positive.

THE KING (*who finds unlimited savor in Pepys*). Well, well, I may be wrong.

PEPYS. The third time it was "my good Mr. Pepys." It was at twenty-seven minutes after four. I noted it by the Strasbourg clock on the chimney piece, so that I might be exact in my report to my wife.

THE KING. Mrs. Pepys, I infer, was unappreciative.

PEPYS (*poignantly*). Mrs. Pepys laughed at me for the value I placed upon your Majesty's condescension. She is a virtuous woman, but she forgot herself.

THE KING (*with assumed gravity*). Ah! You must tell Mrs. Pepys that I am disappointed in her. Tell her that I do not waste my proper names on the husbands of ungrateful women.

PEPYS. I am much obliged to your Majesty. That will be a wholesome chastisement.

THE KING. I fancy Mrs. Pepys would be an amusing

person to know. (*Pepys receives this suggestion with solemnity.*) You shall tell her that.

PEPYS. If I told her that, she would be impossible to live with.

THE KING. It is difficult to turn from so attractive a subject. But we must come to business, Mr. Pepys.

PEPYS (*with eagerness*). The Navy, sir?

THE KING (*rather dumbfounded*). The Navy! The Navy! No. (*He glances at the documents on the table.*) Ah, yes, I forgot. You use business to enliven your amours. Pepys, your mistress is your ledger.

PEPYS. At least she never deceives me.

THE KING (*laughing*). No, because she has no other wooers. For my part, I am quite the opposite to you. I carry amours into estimates. When they talk to me of the price of hemp and the dearth of turpentine, I dream of arms and breasts, the Nereids round the prow.

PEPYS. Your Majesty wished to talk to me of the Nereids?

THE KING. No. And yet, yes. Pepys, each of us expects a lady here tonight.

PEPYS (*never wanting in precision*). Mine is a housemaid.

THE KING. True, true. But that is unimportant. They are both shockingly tardy — tardiness, by-the-by, is quite inexcusable in a housemaid — but they may be upon us at any moment.

PEPYS. Yes, your Majesty.

THE KING (*throwing out his arms, and giving a large-minded sonority to his voice*). What shall we do with them, Pepys? What shall we do with them?

PEPYS. I had forgot.

THE KING. You must admit that the situation is perplexing. I should hate of all things to be inhospitable in my own palace, but it seems clear that our occupations for this evening are — confidential, and that the accommodations (*he waves his arm toward the door back*) are — limited.

PEPYS (*who is slightly but nevertheless sincerely shocked by this*). If I had known —

THE KING (*with his sincere kindness*). Do not distress yourself, my dear fellow. I am an old soldier, Pepys, and am never squeamish about sharing quarters with my friends. But there are women to be considered, and women require explanations. It is very odd: they never give any, but they always want them.

PEPYS (*half rising*). I will go at once.

THE KING (*checking him*). No, no, sit down. We must solve this little puzzle together. As I have said, there are the women. Will they listen to reason? The housemaid may be obliging, but I regret to say that the lady whom I expect seldom listens to anything and never — so far as I know — to reason. No, my dear Pepys. We must face the the facts. We must dismiss — with reluctance, but with finality — the idea of a "quartet."

PEPYS (*turning away his face*). Your Majesty!

THE KING (*not unmoved by the manifest sincerity of Pepys's distress, but not moved quite enough to relinquish his pleasantry*). One of us must give way to the other. I have a great delicacy in asking you to withdraw in my favor, but we kings are a little spoiled, Mr. Pepys. (*As he says this, the King, profligate a moment ago, becomes one of the most teasingly lovable of human beings.*)

PEPYS. It is you who spoil your subjects, sir. (*He rises, and stoops to kiss the King's hand*).

THE KING (*handing Pepys the string of pearls*). We mustn't cheat our housemaid. (*Pepys receives the pearls, deposits them in the box, fetches his cloak and hat from the chair, and drops the box into one*

of the pockets of the cloak.) That is a handsome
cloak of yours.

PEPYS (*modestly*). The outside is well enough.

THE KING. The outside? What is the trouble with
the inside? (*He takes the cloak from Pepys, and
exposes its lining.*) French satin! Really, Mr.
Pepys, I can't imagine what you wear when you
visit countesses.

PEPYS (*modestly beaming*). The lining is quite
worthless, I assure you.

THE KING. I have a fellow-feeling for the worthless,
Pepys. (*He passes his hand in lingering approval
down the glossy lining of the cloak.*) Charming!
It confirms what I often say to myself when I
survey my own defects — that the worthless may
be the charming.

PEPYS. No one who knows your Majesty could doubt
that. (*At this the King's laughter nearly bursts
the dykes, but Pepys remains undisturbed in the
bliss of having said a graceful thing to royalty.
He takes the cloak from the King's extended
hand, and proceeds to gather up the two documents from the desk top.*)

THE KING (*indifferently, as he watches Pepys*). Let
me see that paper for a moment — no, the other

one. I can't read shorthand. (*Pepys, very reluctant, but unable to frame a protest, hands the bulkier manuscript to the King. The King's eye runs lightly along the first page.*)

PEPYS (*nervous*). If your Majesty would be gracious enough to excuse me —

THE KING (*good-naturedly*). Shortly, shortly. (*He lays down the first page upon the desk, and examines the second, still casually.*) This is not your work.

PEPYS. It is my handwriting.

THE KING. But not your composition?

PEPYS (*more and more nervous*). No. May I beg your Majesty's gracious leave to go? Lady Castlemaine may arrive at any moment —

THE KING (*looking up keenly*). *Lady Castlemaine!*

PEPYS. I beg your Majesty's pardon. I thought — (*The King raises his hand with a brief, silencing gesture. He continues to run through the manuscript.*)

THE KING. You don't know who wrote this?

PEPYS. No, sir.

THE KING (*half abstractedly, as he continues his reading*). Who told you Lady Castlemaine was coming here tonight? (*Pepys remains silent.*) The truth — the truth. (*This is said, not roughly, but with a firmness that is irresistible.*)

PEPYS. My Lord Sandwich spoke to me about it.

THE KING (*still busy with the sheets, which he successively takes up and lays down*). This fellow doesn't think so much of my Navy as you do. (*Pause.*) When did my Lord Sandwich tell you this?

PEPYS. This evening, at my house.

THE KING. H-m! Sandwich might mention such a point to Albemarle, and you, I suppose, discuss it with your fellow clerks, but when Sandwich mentioned the matter to you, he forgot himself. One thing further, my dear Pepys. There is a decorum even in scandal, and the names of ladies who visit gentlemen toward the small hours are not to be lightly mentioned — even by his Majesty's most valued clerks. (*He checks Pepys in a movement to reply.*) There, say no more about it. Goodnight. There's your manuscript. (*He hands the manuscript to Pepys; then, with the summary air of one who concludes a tedious subject with a perfunctory question, he says.*) He's wrong, I suppose?

PEPYS. My Lord Sandwich?

THE KING. No, man, no. That fellow. (*He points to the manuscript.*) His story is quite different from yours. I believe you to be an honest servant of the Crown, and you should know the facts better than he does. You do think he's wrong?

PEPYS (*in great embarrassment*). Do I think he's wrong?

THE KING. Yes. He must be wrong unless I have been lied to.

PEPYS (*quivering, but resolute*). He isn't wrong, your Majesty.

THE KING. What does this mean?

PEPYS. It means you have been lied to.

THE KING (*a little wearily*). No doubt. I am a king.

PEPYS (*in great agitation*). Your Majesty should know the whole truth.

THE KING (*smiling, but still weary*). I prefer the truth in smaller packages.

PEPYS (*half to the King, half to himself*). There are things a man who loves his King and country *cannot* see done — though he should starve —

THE KING. Most Englishmen contrive to love their King and country without starving.

PEPYS (*not listening but looking fixedly at the King*). But it is hard to starve.

THE KING. There I quite agree with you. But why starve?

PEPYS. My Lord Sandwich will cast me out if I tell your Majesty the truth.

THE KING. Why?

PEPYS (*with a painful effort*). He *will* have the war — he and my Lord Albemarle. Your Majesty does not love war?

THE KING (*more gravely*). There are things certainly that I love better, Pepys. I like blood in a woman's lip or a child's cheek — not on paving stones — or grass — or sea water. The Dutch have their foibles; they are painfully pious and exaggeratedly clean. I can forgive these things at Whitehall; at Breda I must confess that they annoyed me. My subjects, however, appear to have an unconquerable aversion to tulips and scrubbing pails.

PEPYS (*who in his inner struggle has scarcely heard the King*). A man loves his snug little income, his laced coat, his roast, and his glass of sherry after dinner — but — after all — *when England isn't ready —*

THE KING (*quietly*). I thought she was.

PEPYS. You do not know all.

THE KING. Very possibly, but considering everything,

the sacrifices you make, the hour, the place—
(*very smoothly*) my expectations—(*still more smoothly*) and yours, Mr. Pepys, shall we not leave the matter where it stands?

PEPYS. Your Majesty loves England?

THE KING. Not so well as my subjects. For the subject England is a mistress. For the King she is a wife. That is the painful difference.

PEPYS (*dropping on his knee before the King*). Think of her tonight.

THE KING. I wonder if you ever heard the favorite definition of a wife in Versailles? "A wife is a person whom one doesn't think about in her absence."

PEPYS. I have a very bold thing to ask.

THE KING (*a little impatient*). Speak out.

PEPYS (*bending to the earth*). Give the night to me.

THE KING (*dumbfounded*). To you?

PEPYS. My accounts—they are all in the drawer. (*Points to the desk.*) I will confess all the lies— my King shall know the truth.

THE KING. Get up, Pepys. (*Pepys obeys.*) You are very generous, but you forget that I told you I had already made another disposition of my night.

PEPYS (*with something between archness and simplicity*). So had I.

THE KING. I remember. (*Delicately.*) You would give her up for me? I wish that I could take on the virtues of my subjects as readily as they appropriate my faults. But you see, my dear fellow, whatever a clerk may do for a housemaid, it is impossible for a king to disappoint a lady.

PEPYS (*with modest firmness*). The lady is a subject, I presume.

THE KING. Much as you seem to know about my private life, the remark shows that you are unacquainted with the lady. After all, why tonight, Pepys? Why this haste? There is every reason to hope — or fear (*he sighs lightly*) that the sun will rise up on a world which pesters kings with calculations.

PEPYS (*hesitantly*). Tomorrow will be too late.

THE KING. Why?

PEPYS. Lady Castlemaine —

THE KING (*never more winning than in reproof*). I thought there were some names to which we had agreed to be respectful.

PEPYS (*disobeying out of sheer flurry*). Lady Castlemaine is to persuade your Majesty—to go to war—tonight.

THE KING (*rising precipitately*). Upon my word! (*His brow darkens with a wrath at strange menacing variance with his habitual mood of bantering urbanity. But as his ire is about to break upon the quaking Pepys, it is checked in mid-course by a sense of the disproportion between the passion and its object, and the King, after a moment's conflict with himself, is able to speak with an approach to tranquillity.*)

THE KING. Lord Sandwich told you this?

PEPYS. Yes. My lord has told me many things.

THE KING (*half to himself*). Nobles and mistress combine to make a dupe and butt of me. To whom should a king turn?

PEPYS (*summoning all his courage*). To his people, your Majesty.

THE KING. The people, the people. Pepys, you are right. Tonight my rendezvous shall be with England.

PEPYS (*joyfully*). You will listen to me?

THE KING (*still eager, but already a shade more careless*). Till daybreak, if you like. (*Pepys springs toward the desk, opens the drawer, and begins to*

*take out packets of documents. The King looks
at each packet as it emerges with a twinkle which
becomes whimsically rueful as the extraction continues.*)

PEPYS (*having taken out the last packet*). Now, your
Majesty!

THE KING. Where are we to go, Pepys? (*Pepys evidently had not thought of this.*) It is impossible
to remain here and face the Phyllises whom we
are deserting.

PEPYS (*after a moment's thought, pointing to the
door back*). We could use that room. (*The King
begins to smile.*) It has a table.

THE KING. It has a lock. That is more to the purpose.

PEPYS (*impressively*). And double bolts.

THE KING. I shall send the architect a purse. Van-
brugh himself could not have been more far-
seeing. Let us have a look at that door. (*Pepys,
uncertain of the King's drift, follows him to the
door at back center.*)

PEPYS (*placing his hand against the door*). Oak,
sir — massive oak.

THE KING. Excellent. It is not the first time that oak
has protected Charles Stuart.

PEPYS (*who has examined the door carefully*). It is

the same kind of oak which furnishes the hulls for your Majesty's battleships. The veins run fanwise.

THE KING. Naval oak. In that case it should be able to stand assault and battery.

PEPYS. I do not quite follow your Majesty.

THE KING. No; tonight, Pepys, it is your part to lead. However, the door is all that an escaping monarch could wish. Your housemaid is not muscular?

PEPYS (*unenlightened, but truthful*). She is a slight thing.

THE KING. Capital. I had feared that the wielder of a broom in a Dutch Embassy might be dangerous. You expect her to stay here all night?

PEPYS. I had not thought of that.

THE KING. Let us see. She was to take your short-hand manuscript back to the Embassy, was she not? (*Pepys bows.*) She might go if she had the manuscript.

PEPYS (*with sudden shrewdness*). She might sooner go if she had the pearls. (*He draws the box from his pocket, then proceeds to the table, opens the drawer, and puts the box inside it. Then he looks at the King.*) They will be safe?

THE KING (*stroking his beard*). Hardly. A palace is not a sanctuary, and they say that there are pickpockets in St. Paul's. (*Pepys, after a moment's thought, is about to restore the box to his pocket, when the King is struck by an idea.*) Leave the box. That will show her that you have bought the pearls. (*Pepys takes the pearls from the box, puts them into his pocket, and puts back the box into the drawer. Then he puts the shorthand manuscript into the drawer.*)

PEPYS (*gathering up the other documents*). Now for these.

THE KING (*nearing the door, and pausing to survey the room*). Pardon the caution of a restored monarch, Mr. Pepys, but your cloak and hat — (*Pepys picks up cloak and hat from chair.*) At Worcester, you see, I learned to leave as few clews as possible in the route of a pursuing enemy. I am a fugitive by trade, my Pepys. (*Takes Pepys's arm.*) — If we get out of this alive, you shall tell your wife that I called you "my Pepys" — as I was saying I am a fugitive by trade, but hitherto mostly from husbands, who have a most illogical way of defending the property which they do not value. But this affair tonight is the most singular amorous adventure in which I have ever engaged. The sight of Lady Castlemaine's face when she sees who has tempted me from her side, what has replaced her in the *cubiculum,* would be worth a whole comedy by Etherege. I wish he were here; I shall need him — (*he half yawns, half checks a yawn, and turns on Pepys the demure twinkle of a self-commiserating eye*) before daybreak. You first; I trust no one to lock that door but me. Come on! This night we shall be closeted with England. (*They enter the rear room, Pepys first. The noise of securing the door may be exaggerated and prolonged if the audience prove on experiment to be amused by the idea of masculine safeguards against feminine invasion.*

The stage is empty for some seconds; then a knock is heard at the door right, then a second and third. The door is cautiously opened from without, and Anne looks in. Her person follows her glance; after a brief survey, she speaks to some one in the corridor without.)

ANNE. He isn't here, ma'am.

MRS. PEPYS (*without*). Is nobody there?

ANNE. Nobody. (*With a sense of secret frolic.*) Come in.

MRS. PEPYS (*entering by the door that Anne holds open, and looking round with much perplexity*).

Where can he be? (*Anne passes behind the screen. Mrs. Pepys looks at her inquiringly, as she reappears. Anne shakes her head.*) After all, then, he didn't care much. (*She says this half to herself, with evident relief. Anne looks pointedly at the door back. Mrs. Pepys, observing Anne, looks at the door with an attempt at philosophical detachment. Then the two women look at each other.*)

ANNE (*defensively*). I never said he was in there, ma'am.

MRS. PEPYS (*kind, but peremptory, after her fashion*). Certainly not. Mr. Pepys is a methodical man. He is almost too methodical. If he told you to come here at eleven o'clock for a paper — for a paper, you understand —

ANNE (*with impressive innocence*). For a paper, yes, ma'am.

MRS. PEPYS. He wouldn't go to bed till he had given you the paper. He's stepped out for a minute. (*She says this with a condescending air of large finality.*)

ANNE (*with hypocritical conviction*). That's just what he's done. (*She continues, however, to stare fixedly at the door back.*)

MRS. PEPYS. I suppose we may sit down while we

wait for Mr. Pepys. (*Anne waits with pointed deference till Mrs. Pepys has seated herself on sofa, then turns a chair round so that it exactly faces the door back, and sits down. She stares at the door like a judge at a criminal from whom a belated confession is expected.*)

MRS. PEPYS (*annoyed, but dignified*). We aren't watching that door, you know, Anne.

ANNE. I beg your pardon, ma'am. (*She rises, turns the chair round, and sits down again in such a fashion that the chair is now within two feet of the door. Pause.*)

MRS. PEPYS (*in a pensive, detached way*). You don't — hear anything?

ANNE (*warming instantly to the new humanity in Mrs. Pepys*). No, ma'am, not a sound.

MRS. PEPYS (*waving a repressive hand*). It doesn't matter. It just occurred to me.

ANNE. I don't blame you, ma'am. It happens to the best of us. (*Mrs. Pepys stares hard at Anne. Then she directs a look of virtuous expectation toward the door right; Anne's look, garbing itself in the same virtue, takes the same direction. Pause of several seconds.*)

MRS. PEPYS (*for the sake of breaking the tension*). He will come — very soon.

ANNE (*with a slight backward gesture*). I might — peek in.

MRS. PEPYS (*with firm sweetness*). No, Anne. We will remember, if you please, who we are, and where we are.

ANNE. Not one *little* peek?

MRS. PEPYS. I forbid you to do anything of the kind. (*Pause.*) Of course, Anne, if you chose to disobey me, I suppose there is nothing I could do to prevent you.

ANNE (*after digesting this*). Do you want me to disobey you, ma'am?

MRS. PEPYS (*severely*). No, indeed. I should certainly never forgive you — unless I was convinced that you were truly sorry. (*Anne rises, turns, and applies her eye to the keyhole; then she turns a look of baffled enterprise on Mrs. Pepys. She then lowers her eye to the doorsill.*)

ANNE. There's a light — candles.

MRS. PEPYS (*discarding virtue*). Is that all?

ANNE. That's all that I can see.

MRS. PEPYS (*resuming virtue in her discontent with*

the rewards of wickedness). I am very glad that you can see nothing whatever, Anne.

ANNE. I can hear a voice, I think — I *think* — it's Mr. Pepys's.

MRS. PEPYS. No other voice? Listen carefully. It might be a low voice — a very gentle voice — you know.

ANNE (*lavishly perceptive*). Oh yes, I understand that. (*She tries again, twice, three times.*) It's no use. *She* isn't talking.

MRS. PEPYS (*suddenly resolute*). You may get up, Anne. (*Anne gets up, as Mrs. Pepys leaves the sofa.*) I shall knock upon that door. Sit down, Anne. (*Anne moves with extreme reluctance to the sofa vacated by Mrs. Pepys. Mrs. Pepys knocks — a crisp, short knock. No response. Another quick, crisp knock. No response. Mrs. Pepys looks at Anne.*)

ANNE (*glad of a subject on which she can tutor the authoritative Mrs. Pepys*). Bless you, ma'am. *They* don't want *us*.

MRS. PEPYS (*decided even in surrender*). I don't dare knock again. Anne, we must go home.

ANNE (*dubiously*). I can't go home without the paper.

MRS. PEPYS (*resourceful after a moment's discomfiture*). Mr. Pepys would not forget that paper. If he has not taken it to the Embassy himself, he has left it here for you. Look in the drawer. (*Anne opens drawer, and produces manuscript.*) There! I told you that my husband forgets nothing. Is there anything else in the drawer?

ANNE (*producing box*). This, ma'am. (*She hands the box to Mrs. Pepys.*) I thought it might be — since he never forgets anything —

MRS. PEPYS (*very crisply*). To be sure. If this box contains your pearls, you shall have them. (*She opens the box, which contains only silver paper.*) It is empty — you see. (*The triumph in her face gradually lessens, as she watches the growing mortification in Anne's.*)

ANNE (*nodding toward the back door*). He's given them to *her*. I won't go, ma'am. (*She thrusts the manuscript back into the drawer, which she brusquely closes.*) She shan't have my pearls.

MRS. PEPYS. You think so? I shan't go either. She shan't have my husband. (*The two women, in incongruous fellowship, stand together looking sternly at the door back. Suddenly a sound as of the tentative and circumspect turning of a door*

*knob makes itself heard from another quarter,
the door right.*) Someone is coming. Mr. Pepys?

ANNE (*looking toward the door back with a por-
tentously sagacious headshake*). Not Mr. Pepys,
ma'am.

MRS. PEPYS. Then we must hide. This way. (*She
hurries Anne behind the sofa where the two
women crouch together. The door right is cautiously opened to admit the Queen of England.
She is quite alone, and her slight, but shapely,
figure is clothed in a black gown to which a thick
white scarf, coiled around the neck and dropping
one loose end far down the back, supplies the only
contrast. Her face is meager, but not unhand-
some; its hue is chocolate. She is a quick-moving
woman, with strong temperamental contrasts of
an undemonstrative kind; the two oftenest mani-
fested in the following dialogue are shy rashness
and rueful gayety.*)

THE QUEEN (*looking round the seemingly empty
room*). No? (*She moves left so that she may look
behind the screen.*) No? (*She returns, looks
toward the door back, glides noiselessly toward it,
turns the handle of the door with extreme caution.
After two or three trials, she heaves a little pouting*

sigh, then gives the floor a tiny stamp with a tiny foot.) Too late. (*The Queen's accent is still more foreign than her slightly foreign English.*) H—m! (*Her attention has been caught by an indiscreet movement from Anne. She moves right, and discovers Anne and Mrs. Pepys, who rise in confusion from their place of hiding.*) Ah! There are people here? Who are you?

MRS. PEPYS (*with an embarrassed courtesy*). I am Mrs. Pepys, and this is my—my husband's messenger.

THE QUEEN (*stammering*). P—p—pys! That is too short. I cannot wind my tongue round it. Why are you here now?

MRS. PEPYS. I am waiting for my husband. He has been using this room as an office for a few days. He is a clerk in the Navy.

THE QUEEN. I have a husband, too, but he is not a clerk. You see, Madam, there are not clerks enough to go round. Sit down. (*She seats herself on the sofa, and invites Mrs. Pepys to take the seat beside her. Mrs. Pepys hesitates.*) Do not fear. It is true I am the Queen, but it shall be a secret between us.

MRS. PEPYS (*thunderstruck*). The Queen!

THE QUEEN (*insistently*). Sit down. The messenger will not speak of it. She shall sit down, too, and then she will not tattle. (*Mrs. Pepys and Anne, in obedience to gestures from the Queen, both sit down, Anne behind the sofa.*) I have no chance to talk to pleasant women. The serving maids are rather stupid. One might almost better talk to peeresses.

MRS. PEPYS. I do not know how I should talk to a queen.

THE QUEEN. That is good. That will let me do all the talking. This husband of yours with his bumpy English name — you love him?

MRS. PEPYS (*shy, but resolute*). Very much.

THE QUEEN. And he loves you?

MRS. PEPYS (*with the faintest side glance at Anne*). I hope so.

THE QUEEN (*pensively*). Hope is a pleasant thing. (*Pause.*) It came with me to England, but — I think it has gone back to Portugal. It did not like the English air. What is your husband doing in this place?

MRS. PEPYS. He draws up papers for the King — to show what the Navy could do in a Dutch war.

THE QUEEN. Does he want war — your husband?

MRS. PEPYS (*hesitating between loyalty to Pepys and the desire to rival him in influence upon the mind of royalty*). I think not. He often quotes Lord Southampton who said that if anybody wanted a shovel to dig graves with the plague would serve his turn quite as well as a war.

THE QUEEN. The King would like that. He is very good-natured — the King. He would have no blood shed, no, nor tears either, in his kingdom. But (*she drops her voice*) they are shed — sometimes.

MRS. PEPYS. But then, if the King is so peaceable, we shall have no war.

THE QUEEN (*shrugging her little shoulder*). Who can say? The King is too peaceable to fight with the men who want war. And then there are the women. (*She allows her eyes to rest pointedly on the door back.*) I think we shall have a war.

MRS. PEPYS (*timidly*). Do you like the Dutch, Madam?

THE QUEEN. Oh, yes, the Dutch have a good hate for the Spaniards. In that they are good Portuguese.

MRS. PEPYS (*willing to exalt herself in the Queen's eyes*). Mr. Pepys talked to the King for three hours today.

THE QUEEN. Figures?

MRS. PEPYS. Yes.

THE QUEEN. The King says that when people talk
figures to him, his mind is all sixes and sevens.
That is a joke, is it? They all laughed.

MRS. PEPYS (*laughing, but discreetly tempering her
laugh*). He is amusing.

THE QUEEN. He loves a pleasant word. He is fond of
pleasure. He said the other day that a throne
should have a cushion. Lord Halifax said there
was more cushion than throne. I laughed at that,
but not much. It is best to laugh gently at kings.

MRS. PEPYS. I should never laugh at a king, or at a
queen either.

THE QUEEN. For kings, yes, that is right. But as for
queens, I do not know. They are very much like
women. The lapdogs do not even know the difference. (*A knock is heard at the door right. The
Queen instantly rises; the others follow her example.*) Who is that? Come with me. (*She leads
Mrs. Pepys and Anne to the space behind the
screen, where motioning her companions to withdraw toward the left, the Queen takes her stand
as near as possible to the door back. Enter from
the door right Lady Castlemaine, an imperious*

and insolent beauty, clad in a sweeping dressing gown of costly material and sumptuous color. She grasps the emptiness of the visible part of the room in a single sweepingly inclusive glance. Without hesitation she advances toward the door back, lowers her mouth to the keyhole, and speaks in a low but richly penetrating voice.)

LADY CASTLEMAINE. Charles! (*Silence. Lady Castlemaine, not venturing a second call, draws a key from her bodice, inserts it in the lock, and is beginning to turn it with manifest effort when the Queen steps out from behind the screen. The Queen's face is alive with an exultant discovery which almost overpowers her efforts to mask her feeling and to speak with limpidly ironic sympathy.*)

THE QUEEN. You are late, Castlemaine. The King is — occupied. (*The key drops from Lady Castlemaine's fingers to the floor. She is a woman without fears or scruples, and would have been capable ordinarily of beating or clamoring her way into the presence of the King and her imagined rival, but for the moment she cannot face the humiliation of being visibly supplanted under the eyes of the demurely sardonic Queen. The restraint which she is obliged to put upon her rage augments that rage to a pitch where it is scarcely bearable.*)

LADY CASTLEMAINE. Madam, why are you here? (*The Queen does not answer this; on the contrary, Queen though she is, she stoops and picks up the fallen key.*)

THE QUEEN (*offering the key*). Your key. You may like to keep it — for a *memento.* (*Lady Castlemaine for an instant seems about once more to plunge the key into the lock in contempt of malignant possibilities, but something in the cool irony of the Queen's act is too strong even for her frenzy.*)

LADY CASTLEMAINE (*bitingly*). Thank you. It will be useful, Madam, *still.* (*The "still" is a taunt.*)

THE QUEEN (*liquidly*). All things are possible.

LADY CASTLEMAINE. Not all things, Madam. It is impossible that your Majesty should remain in this place at this hour.

THE QUEEN. I am in my own palace.

LADY CASTLEMAINE. *That* is the danger. You might meet in these rooms the most scandalous persons.

THE QUEEN (*looking steadily at Lady Castlemaine*). I can meet them — in my own apartments.

LADY CASTLEMAINE. The King, Madam, if here, would add his entreaties to mine.

THE QUEEN. I will take the King's wishes from the King's mouth. (*With a half sigh.*) He is not afraid to utter them.

LADY CASTLEMAINE. Look upon that door, Madam, and remember that you are Queen of England.

THE QUEEN. We are on the virtuous side of that door tonight — I and you. We are only too secure, my Castlemaine.

LADY CASTLEMAINE (*pricked beyond self-control*). Madam, *who* is with the King?

THE QUEEN. Who? I do not know. I am curious, like you. We grow sisterly, do we not?

LADY CASTLEMAINE. This is past bearing. Where is that key? (*She is about to thrust the key into the lock when the Queen speaks with subdued authority.*)

THE QUEEN. If *I* can wait, Castlemaine — (*Lady Castlemaine's eyes dart venom, but again the situation is coercive. She replaces the key in her gown.*)

LADY CASTLEMAINE. Shall you wait till — morning?

THE QUEEN. I do not know. It is true we need our sleep, Castlemaine, you and I. We reach a time when—what do you call them?—restoratives are needful. These kings are so sharp-sighted.

LADY CASTLEMAINE. These remarks may be comic in Portugal. But what will the King say when he opens the door and finds his Queen upon the threshold?

THE QUEEN (*with a low laugh*). That will be amusing. He will have to apologize—to both of us.

LADY CASTLEMAINE (*broodingly, lost in her own thoughts*). We shall know at least who the trull is.

THE QUEEN. That is the name for women who steal a king's love?

LADY CASTLEMAINE (*much at a loss*). Yes. No. We call them many names.

THE QUEEN. She is young—do you not think so?—very young—and blond. These kings are so changeable. They tire of dark hair.

LADY CASTLEMAINE (*to herself*). If I thought—

THE QUEEN. Patience, patience, Castlemaine. We shall find a refuge. There are convents in Europe—if you would but turn Catholic—which take in women who are past their prime. I know some very handsome abbesses in Oporto.

LADY CASTLEMAINE. No doubt your Portuguese wines turn to vinegar, Madam. In England we have other ferments. You insist on staying here, Madam?

THE QUEEN. I think so.

LADY CASTLEMAINE. In that case it is my plain duty to stay with you. (*She seats herself on the sofa.*) The company of your lady in waiting will lessen the scandal which your Majesty, I regret to say, is certain to incur.

THE QUEEN. You are kind. I am kind, too. If I am here, Castlemaine, nobody will ask why you came or why you stayed.

LADY CASTLEMAINE. Let the nobodies ask questions. That is their business.

THE QUEEN. The trouble is that they answer their own questions.

LADY CASTLEMAINE. It will be a tedious night, Madam.

THE QUEEN. We shall entertain each other.

LADY CASTLEMAINE. At this hour even your Majesty will find it difficult to entertain me.

THE QUEEN. Never mind. There are some other people here.

LADY CASTLEMAINE (*aghast*). Other people!

THE QUEEN. Behind the screen. (*Speaking behind the screen to Anne and Mrs. Pepys.*) Come out!

(*Mrs. Pepys and Anne cautiously show themselves at back center.*)

LADY CASTLEMAINE (*bounding indignantly to her feet*). Who are these — animals? (*The last word is ejected like an execration.*)

THE QUEEN. They are women, I think. At least they are waiting for a man.

LADY CASTLEMAINE. For a man. Of course. What else should such riffraff wait for? (*Mrs. Pepys turns away indignantly.*)

THE QUEEN (*to Mrs. Pepys*). You will not mind Lady Castlemaine. She is waiting for a man, too. Indeed, so am I. (*Then in her half artless, half guileful way.*) It is not a lucky night for the women.

LADY CASTLEMAINE. Madam, who is this woman?

THE QUEEN. She is under my protection, Castlemaine. If you are a little decent to her, you will be very kind to me. She is the wife of a clerk in the Navy. She has a jolly little name, but it swims about in my mouth and I cannot bring it to shore. (*To Mrs. Pepys.*) What is it?

MRS. PEPYS. Pepys, if your Majesty pleases, and (*with an edge in her quiet voice*) — if it pleases Lady Castlemaine.

LADY CASTLEMAINE. The man who talked to the King for three hours today?

THE QUEEN. That is the man. She loves him, and she hopes he loves her. That is much for an Englishwoman.

LADY CASTLEMAINE (*turning her head toward Anne, who has moved to upstage right*). And who is this? (*Mrs. Pepys seems disposed to an offended silence, but a look of expectation from the Queen obliges her to reconsider.*)

MRS. PEPYS. A messenger who is to carry a paper from my husband to the Dutch Embassy.

LADY CASTLEMAINE (*still looking at Anne*). The Dutch Embassy is inexperienced. A homelier messenger of another sex would be much safer from interruption in the streets at midnight. (*Turning to Mrs. Pepys.*) How long have you been expecting this man?

MRS. PEPYS. An hour perhaps.

LADY CASTLEMAINE. What makes you think he will bring you the paper now?

ANNE. The paper's in the drawer, ma'am. (*Mrs. Pepys's signals have pleaded ineffectually with Anne for silence.*)

LADY CASTLEMAINE (*opening the drawer, and taking*

out the paper). This? (*Anne nods. Lady Castlemaine stares baffled at the shorthand; then she turns to Mrs. Pepys.*) If you have the paper, what are you waiting for? (*Mrs. Pepys maintains a troubled silence.*)

ANNE (*sincerely wishing to help Mrs. Pepys*). We're waiting for my pearls. (*Mrs. Pepys shivers a little.*)

LADY CASTLEMAINE. Ah-h-h-h! What Mr. Pepys wants of you is clear. I have one more question, however: What does Mrs. Pepys want of you?

ANNE. She will make him give me the pearls.

LADY CASTLEMAINE. Indeed! The wives of the clerks in his Majesty's Navy are certainly obliging. (*To Mrs. Pepys.*) Is this true?

MRS. PEPYS (*indignant at this baiting*). Must I answer, Madam? (*This to the Queen.*)

THE QUEEN. You shall not answer Lady Castlemaine, my dear, if you do not wish to. But I also am curious. Perhaps you will answer me.

MRS. PEPYS (*after a pause*). I *did* mean that she should have the pearls.

THE QUEEN. But not the man?

MRS. PEPYS (*in her crisp way*). Not if I could stop her.

LADY CASTLEMAINE. In other words, he was to furnish the pearls with which you bribed her to leave him. (*This is not the exact truth, but is so diabolically like the truth that for the moment it quite robs Mrs. Pepys of speech.*)

THE QUEEN (*sorry for Mrs. Pepys*). You do not understand these wives, Castlemaine.

LADY CASTLEMAINE. I am a wife myself.

THE QUEEN. True. I am forgetful. A wife *on leave,* as they say in the Navy.

LADY CASTLEMAINE (*to Mrs. Pepys, pursuing her advantage*). Where is this Pepys? (*Mrs. Pepys is silent, looking, with some entreaty, at the Queen.*)

ANNE (*pointing to the door back*). He is in there. (*The Queen and Lady Castlemaine look at the door back, then at Anne, then at each other.*)

LADY CASTLEMAINE (*to Anne*). Alone? (*Anne drops her eyes.*)

THE QUEEN (*again in her half sly, half artless way*). She is very much shocked. She is a good girl. (*To Mrs. Pepys.*) You think your husband is in there?

MRS. PEPYS (*faltering*). I *did* think so.

THE QUEEN. The room is extraordinarily attractive for husbands. And who do you think is with him? (*Looking toward Anne.*) It can hardly be this young girl whose virtue is so manifest.

MRS. PEPYS. I do not know who is with him.

LADY CASTLEMAINE. My good woman, I have the best of reasons for knowing that this Pepys whom you are looking for is not in that room. If he were, this would be no place for you.

THE QUEEN (*smiling*). Perhaps you will tell her why, Castlemaine.

LADY CASTLEMAINE. Her Majesty wishes me to tell you that when the husband is abroad —

THE QUEEN (*in a rueful parenthesis*). When the wife is foreign, the husband is always abroad.

LADY CASTLEMAINE. The wife forgets her dignity — am I not right, your Majesty? — abases herself when she intrudes into his private pleasures. Let her keep her place at home by the fire —

THE QUEEN (*still rueful and still parenthetic*). Or by the ashes —

LADY CASTLEMAINE. And await his return when he has the leisure to take thought of her.

THE QUEEN. He will take her to mass on Sunday. Mass is very convenient. The husband need not talk to the wife, and the wife cannot talk to the husband.

LADY CASTLEMAINE. The thing for you to do is to take this girl — since you are so strangely fond of her society — and be gone. If the husband or the pearls show themselves, they shall be sent after you.

THE QUEEN. You go too fast, Castlemaine. Let them stay. They are curious. Well, are we not curious? We all want to know, do we not? (*The four women stand at various points surveying the door back.*) It is a long time till morning, and they will amuse us.

LADY CASTLEMAINE. Your Majesty, I hope, does not purpose to spend the night in conversing with these women?

THE QUEEN. Their tongues are like ours. Why not? But if you do not wish to talk, Castlemaine, we will do something else. We will play cards.

LADY CASTLEMAINE. There are no cards here, Madam.

THE QUEEN. There are always cards in Whitehall. (*She turns to Anne.*) My dear, go to that press over there (*she points to the cupboard at left front*) and fetch me a pack of cards. You are to find them, mind. If you do not find them, I shall tell your Mr. Pepys — if it is Mr. Pepys — that you are too stupid to wear pearls. (*Anne goes to the cupboard, opens it, and peers into its dusky contents.*) Let me see. There are four of us. We can play quadrille.

LADY CASTLEMAINE (*with hauteur*). I beg your Majesty's pardon, there are *two* of us.

THE QUEEN. My dear Castlemaine, since I wish to play quadrille, and since two people cannot play quadrille, it is evident that there must be four of us.

ANNE. The cards, your Majesty.

THE QUEEN. Thank you. Do you play quadrille?

ANNE. With the footmen sometimes — and the other housemaids.

THE QUEEN. Very good. You, too, Mrs. Pepys? (*Mrs. Pepys courtesies an affirmative.*) The vices make us all neighborly. There is a card table behind the screen. We shall see the door when it opens. Mrs. Pepys, you shall play with me — the two wives against the two — other ladies. Come. (*They pass behind the screen, and seat themselves at the table.*) Begin. I have a fancy that it is the wives who win tonight. (*She takes up the cards as she glances toward the door.*)

CURTAIN

❁

SCENE III

The curtain rises after forty seconds on the same setting. It is now four o'clock on the morning of the next day. The Queen and Lady Castlemaine are still at the card table playing with the persistence of mechanisms. But Mrs. Pepys and Anne are now on the sofa, Mrs. Pepys sitting upright, while the head of the drowsy Anne has fallen sideways into her companion's not inhospitable lap. For some seconds the stillness is unbroken, then a faint noise as of chairs moving on wood is heard from behind the dulling thickness of the massive door.

THE QUEEN (*pausing in her play, and holding up a finger*). Hush!

LADY CASTLEMAINE (*listening*). They are moving. (*She puts down her cards.*)

THE QUEEN (*also putting down her cards*). We shall know—now. (*Both rise. They look at each other. Bitter as are the divisions between them, common weariness and common expectation establish a brief comradeship between them.*)

LADY CASTLEMAINE. Shall we meet him here?

THE QUEEN (*thoughtfully*). He will be displeased with us.

LADY CASTLEMAINE. I shall be displeased with him. (*But the tone is somewhat less confident than the words.*)

THE QUEEN. Come. (*They move to a point down stage left, from which the door is plainly visible, and seat themselves. A key turns audibly in the lock. The door creaks on its heavy hinges.*)

MRS. PEPYS (*to Anne*). Wake. Sit up. Sit up, I tell you. They are coming. (*Anne sits up and rubs her eyes. The door slowly opens, and the King appears.*)

THE KING (*weary, but still his bland and tranquil self, as his eyes fall on Mrs. Pepys and Anne*). We are expected, Pepys. Come out, and make your apologies.

MRS. PEPYS (*thunderstricken*). The King! (*She rises to her feet and makes an agitated courtesy. Anne remains on the sofa. The King, stepping sideways toward Mrs. Pepys, allows to the emergent Pepys the central position in the doorway. The effect of his appearance on the Queen and Lady Castlemaine is electrical. The slight cry which neither can restrain reaches the King's ears; he turns his head and recognizes the two women; in three rapid moments he assimilates the three*

facts — the Queen, the mistress, and their anoma-
lous companionship. His first impulse is to break
into indignant speech; his second to inflict upon
both women the chastening slight of postponing
them to the persons at his elbow. Pepys, mean-
while, has come forward; he recognizes his wife
with great astonishment, and Anne, a moment
later, with a little less.)

PEPYS. Wife!

MRS. PEPYS. Yes, Pepys.

THE KING. Do not be surprised, Pepys. Wives are omnipresent. Madam, it is I who have parted your husband from you for a night. In seeing you, I can measure his sacrifice.

MRS. PEPYS (*blushing*). Your Majesty.

PEPYS. But, wife, what brings you to Whitehall?

MRS. PEPYS (*pointing to Anne*). I brought *her*. She did not know her way.

PEPYS (*looking at Anne*). Yes, yes, I had forgot.

THE KING. You see, Mrs. Pepys, he has to be re-minded of her existence. Your husband is equally devoted to two things — to England and to his wife. (*Pause.*) In both he is a pattern for his King.

MRS. PEPYS. Your Majesty is too good to him.

THE KING (*with mock gravity*). Am I? Haven't you found him a good husband?

MRS. PEPYS (*with the faintest sidelong glance toward Anne*). Mostly.

THE KING. Mostly? But, my dear Mrs. Pepys, (*Mrs. Pepys looks at Pepys with triumphant emphasis*) what would you have? We men never push sainthood too far. If we were saintly, we should have a reason the less for worshiping our wives.

PEPYS (*taking his wife's arm, with much confidence*). We are a most happy couple, your Majesty.

MRS. PEPYS (*no longer frightened at the gracious King*). Oh, are we, Mr. Pepys?

PEPYS (*conclusively*). We are.

THE KING (*more seriously*). I believe you are. (*More seriously still.*) I wonder — I wonder — if I had been a clerk — (*he looks toward the Queen, but his glance falls upon Lady Castlemaine*) — but let that pass. Go home, Pepys, and be happy, and if the sinful may advise the virtuous, let this sleepy little siren keep the tempting roses in her cheeks to — to brighten the Dutch Embassy.

PEPYS. The Dutch are very fond of flowers.

THE KING. True. We must respect the Dutch. They

are good people, and there is no immediate hurry about fighting them. We have an excellent Navy — so I am told by my Lord Sandwich and my Lord Albemarle — but for the moment we will leave the Dutch — unannihilated. In this point your husband agrees with me, Mrs. Pepys. He has been agreeing with me for five hours. I wish I could turn his broadsides upon the Dutch admirals. I should not hesitate to go to war tomorrow.

PEPYS. Your Majesty will forgive a tiresome subject. I had good reasons enough for holding my tongue, my bit of bread and my roll of stock and my good wife here — but my country tugged at my heart, and I spoke, even while I chid myself for speaking.

THE KING. My dear Pepys, you shall be protected. I am sure there is no public servant who is better informed or less disposed to withhold his information from his sovereign. If you have trouble at the office, report to me. Little as I care to remind my subjects of unpleasant truths, I might go so far as to remind my Lord Sandwich that I am King of England. I shall remember this night sometimes when I wish to think that I deserve the title.

PEPYS. You are always that in the hearts of faithful
subjects. (*They kiss the King's hands.*)

THE KING. Goodnight, Pepys—or is it good morning? Au revoir, Mrs. Pepys. I know just enough
of your courtly tongue to assure a charming
woman that I hope again to meet her. (*He turns,
and moves left toward the Queen and Lady Castlemaine.*)

LADY CASTLEMAINE (*restrained by the Queen's presence, and half appeased by the discovery that the
King's companion was not a rival*). Your Majesty
is an early riser.

THE KING. I wished to be the first to applaud the
same virtue in Lady Castlemaine. (*He bends with
an ironic exaggeration of gallantry to kiss her
hand, then lifting his head, examines her face
critically.*) Madam, you are superb. The hours
that lay waste the rest of us only replenish you.
(*The irony of his tone is unmistakable, and receives a further emphasis from the easy friendli-
ness of tone and gesture with which the King
turns to offer his arm to his wife. They imply all
that easy intimacy which is really not the fact between them.*)

THE KING. Madam, shall we go? (*The Queen, after*

an instant's glance toward Lady Castlemaine, takes the King's proffered arm, and they go out left. The slight to Lady Castlemaine is bitter beyond endurance. She stands truculently silent for twenty seconds till her amassed wrath, famished for an object, suddenly looses itself upon the luckless Pepys, who chances to be equally prominent in her field of vision and in her furious memory.)

LADY CASTLEMAINE *(crossing the stage right toward Pepys, and concentrating her fury in one vitriolic word).* Filth! *(She turns, and goes out by door left. Pepys and his wife look at each other.)*

MRS. PEPYS. She is a foul-mouthed woman, Pepys. Do not heed her.

PEPYS. Foul-mouthed, maybe, but that will not keep the King from giving ear to her.

MRS. PEPYS. But the King snubbed her just now.

PEPYS *(with marked significance).* It's morning now.

MRS. PEPYS. Fie, Pepys!

PEPYS. Things are what they are, wife, though we say "Fie, fie" till doomsday. All men know what the King is among the women. I see not why our mouths should be so dainty when the rest of us has so little mind to be clean.

MRS. PEPYS. Pepys, today you have done a great deed for England, and you shall not be sorry for it.

PEPYS (*wilfully*). I *am* sorry for it. Fool that I was, to help England and forget that I was doing an ill turn to one Samuel Pepys whom I care so much more for. Not to mention the said Samuel Pepys's wife, who is a good little woman, though foolish.

MRS. PEPYS. You would not do the same thing again?

PEPYS. I swear I wouldn't; it is odd how a grown man in his right mind can be taken sometimes with these fits of virtue. Not that it would not be good to stop a bad war if a man could do it without crossing Lady Castlemaine.

MRS. PEPYS. The King will protect you. The King is a great man.

PEPYS. Yes. As soon as he calls a giddy woman "my dear Mrs. Pepys," he is a great man. But we must get home. Can you wake that girl?

MRS. PEPYS (*shaking Anne*). Anne! Anne! Wake up!

PEPYS. The girl is a log. Say "pearls" to her, wife.

MRS. PEPYS. Pearls, Anne, pearls!

ANNE (*instantly awake*). Yes, Mrs. Pepys.

PEPYS. There are the pearls, girl. They are a present from — Mrs. Pepys. (*Gives her the pearls.*)

ANNE. Oh, thank you, ma'am.

MRS. PEPYS. You must come to see me, Anne, and show me how they look on you — some day when Mr. Pepys is at the office.

PEPYS (*who has fetched the shorthand manuscript from the desk drawer*). We will take you to the Embassy, and you must put this paper back in its place.

ANNE. Yes, Mr. Pepys.

PEPYS (*going toward the door back, as the three prepare to leave*). It has been a great night — a night with my King. I am a foolish fellow without wit enough to hold my wagging tongue. God keep me from ever so forgetting myself again! And yet — and yet — the ships *were* rotten, and I had to let him know.

CURTAIN